I WILL BE A DOCTOR!

The Story of America's First Woman Physician

by
DOROTHY CLARKE WILSON

ABINGDON PRESS

Nashville

I Will Be a Doctor!

Library of Congress Cataloging in Publication Data

WILSON, DOROTHY CLARK.
    I will be a doctor!
    Bibliography: p.
    Summary: A biography of the first woman doctor empha-
sizing the hardships she endured in becoming a doctor and in
practicing medicine.
    1. Blackwell, Elizabeth, 1821-1910—Juvenile literature. 2.
Physicians—New York (State)—Biography—Juvenile literature. 3. Women physicians—New York (State)—Biography—
Juvenile literature. [1. Blackwell, Elizabeth, 1821-1910. 2.
Women physicians. 3. Physicians] I. Title.
    R154.B623W48 1983   610'.92'4 [B] [92]   83-3862

ISBN 0-687-19727-9

Acknowledgment is made to Little, Brown and Company, Boston,
publisher in 1970 of the author's book, *Lone Woman,* for permission to
publish this adaptation of the story for young people. An abridged
version appeared in the *Reader's Digest* Condensed Books in 1970.

MANUFACTURED IN THE UNITED STATES OF AMERICA

CONTENTS

1

THE LITTLE BLACK BOOK

"**E**-liz-a-beth. E-liz-a-beth Blackwell."

Peering at her face in the big mahogany mirror, she spoke her name slowly, emphasizing the harsh explosive z's and b's. Then she mouthed the names of other members of her family, "Anna," "Marianne," her two older sisters; "Hannah," her mother; "Samuel," the name of both her father and baby brother; her four aunts, "Ann," "Lucy," "Mary," and "Barbara."

"Bar-ba-ra." She scowled. Only she and her bossy aunt had first names that were different, sharp like the rap of Aunt Bar's ruler on her hand when she had been naughty. All the rest sounded soft and gentle, like most of their faces.

Was her face different, too? Perching on her toes, she leaned forward and looked hard at it. The soft fine hair was not curly and glossy like Anna's. It hung straight as straw and was almost as pale. The cheeks were too thin, mouth too wide, chin too square. The eyes, a clear bluish-gray, stared back at her from under heavy brows, pitilessly honest.

No, she was not pretty like Anna and Marianne, and certainly not beautiful like Mamma, who was lovelier than either of them. She was the odd one, in looks as well as in name.

Suddenly another face appeared in the mirror above hers, grim and threatening. She must be imagining it. Aunt Bar was busy in the kitchen directing work for the big company dinner to-night. Just to prove it wasn't real, she leaned forward and stuck out her tongue at it. Then as a firm hand seized her shoulder, her heart sank. It was real, all right. In dumb misery she watched the hated black book come out of Aunt Bar's big white apron pocket.

"So—three black marks against you this time, Miss Bessie. One for disobeying. You are not allowed in the spare room without permission. One for vanity, looking at yourself in the mirror and preening. And the third, the worst, for impudence. Even your indulgent Mamma would not stand for sticking out your tongue at your elders."

"But— I didn't mean—" Words choked in the child's throat. Besides, she had no excuses. She *had* disobeyed. She *had* been impudent. She *had* been looking in the mirror, though not preening. Fear-fully she waited to hear her punishment. Please— let it be just a black mark in the book, even slaps with the ruler, not something that would last all day— and tonight! But it was.

"To the attic with you, young lady, for the rest of the day, then supper and early to bed in your room. And you'd better spend the time praying that you may be cured of such naughtiness."

In spite of her despair she managed to march with dignity from the room, and with head held high climbed the attic stairs. She did not pray. If Mamma had asked her to, she would have; but she was glad to disobey Aunt Bar. Besides, there was no need to be sorry for her sins, the punishment was so terrible. To have to spend the night of the big party in lonely solitude was almost more than she could bear.

At least there were windows in the attic, though she could see little from them except red-tiled roofs and chimney pots. Trees hid the courtyard garden below, but she could hear voices. Mamma and Aunt Lucy were sitting under the may tree. Aunt Lucy was probably sewing as usual, making one of the frocks which Anna and Marianne hated because they were so dowdy. Mamma hired Aunt Lucy to sew because she needed the money. "It will keep you from vanity," she consoled when the older girls protested. Elizabeth did not mind wearing the ugly clothes if it helped gentle, kind Aunt Lucy. She was sorry for all the four unmarried aunts—Papa's sisters—even for Aunt Bar.

Elizabeth shivered, thinking of the grown-up talk she had overheard about unmarried ladies who had no relatives to support them. They had to sew, like Aunt Lucy, or teach other people's children, like Aunt Ann, or be somebody's housekeeper, like Aunt Bar and Aunt Mary. Suppose no man ever wanted her for a wife!

But her present fate was bad enough. Anna's and Marianne's happy voices in the playroom below revived her agony. She could tell from the sounds that they were riding the wonderful new rocking horse. It was as big as a pony, with a real mane and tail, and a handsome red saddle. Anna would be riding, as usual, on top, with Marianne on the end of the rockers behind. And her place on the front part of the rocker would be empty! They were singing verses from Taylor's "Scenes in Foreign Lands" as they slid over the wooden floor.

Suddenly she remembered Anna's telescope! She went into the attic chamber where Anna kept it. It was a beautiful toy spyglass, which Anna had bought for a half crown last summer. How wonderful to have it all to herself! She took it to the window, gasping because it made everything look so big. It seemed almost as if she could see beyond England to the rest of Europe and far away into the East.

Papa had been displeased about the spyglass. The three girls had climbed through the window onto the leads (the flat roof). Sitting behind the parapet, they had looked across the roofs and chimneys of Bristol to the fields and woods beyond. It had been such fun, almost like flying! But Marianne had had to spoil it. Papa had not dubbed her "Monkey Polly" for nothing! Instead of sitting quietly, she had walked the whole length of the roof where there was no parapet, and one of the servants had seen her. Papa had forbidden them to ever climb onto the leads again.

Anna had written a petition, promising that they would sit perfectly still, and they had all signed it. She had carried it to him as he sat at his washstand, shaving. He had read it through, smiling, laid down his razor, taken a pencil from his waistcoat pocket, and written on the back of the petition:

Anna, Bessie and Polly. Your request is mere folly,
The leads are too high   For those who can't fly.
If I let you go there,   I suppose your next prayer
Will be for a hop   To the chimney top!
So I charge you three misses,   Not to show your phizes
On parapet wall,   Or chimney so tall,
But to keep to the earth,   The place of your birth.
"Even so," says Papa. "Amen," says Mamma.
"Be it so," says Aunt Bar.

Wonderful Papa, who unlike Aunt Bar could say no without hurting! Elizabeth's sharp ears caught the sound of his turning latchkey, and her heart lurched. He was coming home early from his sugarhouse. Crouching at the head of the attic stairs, she heard a rush of feet as Anna and Marianne flew to meet him, his hearty voice greeting them.

"Ho, my bonny Anna and Monkey Polly, and young Samuel Charles, what mischief have you been up to today? And where's my Bessie, my Little Shy?"

A low rumble from Aunt Bar detailed the sins recorded in the little black book. Elizabeth tightened her eyelids until they hurt. There would be no leniency from Papa, only tut tuts and "Dear, dear, what a pity!" He never interfered with Aunt Bar's discipline. Shame over Papa's distress at her sins was almost worse then the punishment she must endure.

Jane, one of the housemaids, came to tell her that supper was served in her room, and after eating it she was to go directly to bed. Elizabeth ate without appetite, even though old Margaret the cook had managed to smuggle a few choice bits of meat, fruit, and sweets into the usual prison fare of tea, thick bread, and water.

With her usual neatness she removed her pinafore, her pretty party frock, her petticoats, and white frilled pantalettes, and folded them all carefully. Bleakly she put on her long white nightgown and crawled into bed. But not to sleep! Hours later, it seemed, she tiptoed from her room, sneaked down the stairs, and crouched on one of the steps in the dark, peering through the banister.

She could see into the dining room with its big mahogany table. Dinner was over. The guests were all ministers or missionaries from the religious groups called Dissenters. This meant they did not belong to the Church of England. One of them was telling a funny story, and everybody was laughing—Papa loudest of all. One of the men looked as if he were ready to fall down and roll on the floor. Mamma was laughing until the tears ran down her face. All the aunts, even Aunt Bar, were shaking with laughter and holding handkerchiefs to their faces. And there were Anna and Marianne, sitting at their small table at one side. The third chair, the pretty mahogany child's chair, with its horsehair seat and bar underneath, and a brass screw for making it go up and down, was empty!

The mirror was right. She was different. She was the odd one, the outcast the missionaries told about. She was the sinner thrust into outer darkness. Would she always be different, doing things Aunt Bar didn't approve of, getting herself into all kinds of trouble?

She crept back up the stairs, into her dark room, and climbed into bed.

2

"ONE MAN SHOULDN'T OWN ANOTHER!"

In spite of Aunt Bar and her little black book, Elizabeth's childhood in Bristol, England during the 1820s was a happy one. There were hardships and disappointments. Some, like most of the entries in the black book, were her own fault.

Once when she was a very small child Papa was going on a trip to Dublin, Ireland, and the whole family went down to Hot Springs to see him off on the boat. Elizabeth was sure he was going to take her with him. Then, to her amazement, he said good-bye to her along with the rest. As the boat moved slowly down the river, Elizabeth followed Anna and Marianne as they ran along the bank waving their handkerchiefs. When the vessel moved faster and her sisters stopped, she kept on running.

"What are you trying to do?" screamed Anna, trying vainly to catch up with her. "Do you think you can go with him on foot?"

Elizabeth kept on running. Panting, Anna managed to reach her, seized her by the shoulders, and spun her around, and though five years older, she was no match for Elizabeth in strength.

"Look, silly," she reasoned. "Dublin's in Ireland,

an island with water all around it. You could run a hundred miles and not get to him."

Elizabeth submitted, but sullenly, and spoke not a word all the way home.

"A persistent child," said Aunt Mary, always kind and gentle.

"Stubborn!" snapped Aunt Bar.

Elizabeth worried as more and more of her "sins" were entered in the black book. Sin! She heard about it each Sunday in the chapel, and repentance was harped on every day in family prayers. How could she get rid of her sins? The saints had done so, she read in stories about them, by something called "mortifying the body and despising the flesh." She tried crawling out of bed and sleeping on the floor. Once she even tried to go without food until Aunt Bar decided she was sick and dosed her with physic. But it did no good. Her name kept appearing in the black book.

Elizabeth was definitely not Aunt Bar's favorite among the children. At first Aunt Bar had been partial to Marianne. Then Samuel, a younger brother, had become her pet. But after another son, Henry, usually called Harry, arrived, he became her favorite. She curled his hair every morning with water and a tail comb, and beamed with pride when she took him walking and people stopped to admire him.

Elizabeth could not remember a time in her childhood when Mamma was not nursing a baby. After Harry came two more girls, Emily and Ellen. Elizabeth had come between two boys who had died.

All in twos she thought unhappily. All except herself. Anna and Marianne. Samuel and Harry. Emily and Ellen. It was just one more way that she was different.

Papa, she came to understand, was different, too, from most other Englishmen of his time. It was because of his difference that she and her sisters had a governess who taught them not only to read and write but history and mathematics, and even something called philosophy. She overheard conversations.

"You're a fool, Samuel, to spend all this money teaching your *girls*. The boys, of course, have to be taught to read and write, and add, to run a business."

"Ladies," another might tell him, "should be taught music, painting, embroidery, penmanship, perhaps a bit of French. Those are accomplishments which a lady can always use, whether she gets married or not."

Papa would reply mildly, "My daughters have as good minds as my sons. I see no reason why they should not be taught to use them. As to what use they will put them to in later life, that will be for them to decide."

Papa made life an exciting adventure. Each day, sometimes twice a day, under Papa's orders, the governess would take Elizabeth and her sisters for long walks around Bristol and the surrounding country. Elizabeth enjoyed these excursions. Inside her long skirts and frilled pantalettes her thin legs grew tough and wiry as they moved to the clatter of pattens (shoes with wooden soles) which lifted her feet above the wet flagstones, or to the quieter rhythms of corked clogs. She trudged the narrow cobblestone streets, plodded the roads and paths along the riverbanks to the brook and to St. Vincent's Rocks beyond. In one side of the steep cliff there was a dark cave called the Giant's Hole. While her sisters stood back from the abyss, shuddering, Elizabeth wriggled forward on her stomach and peered over the edge, wishing she were a boy so she could escape from troublesome elders and explore the fascinating depths.

But there was no need of exploring dangerous gullies to find excitement. One day the whole household—Mamma, aunts, children, servants— all except Papa, who was fighting the fire, stood huddled against the railings at the top of Bridge Street, and watched Papa's sugar refinery burn to the ground. Elizabeth could feel the heat on her face, even coursing into her hands as she clung to the railings.

Poor Papa! Not only had he suffered a severe loss, but he must borrow money to provide a new building and equipment. He bought two adjoining houses on Nelson Street; one became the new sugar refinery. To economize, he moved the family into the other. Fiercely independent, he abhorred debts of any kind. And, as Elizabeth well knew, one of the debts he hated most was that of his sugar business. For the sugar cane he must import from Jamaica was raised by slave labor.

"One man shouldn't own another," he often declared aloud.

Perhaps it was John Wesley, the Methodist, who was responsible for Samuel Blackwell's concern about slavery. Nearly a hundred years before, Wesley had come to Bristol to preach. For almost the first time there had been someone to speak for England's poor, the coal-blackened miner, the children spinning cotton for a few pennies a week, and the slaves being brought from Africa for sale. As a result the slave trade had been abolished in England in 1807, fourteen years before Elizabeth was born, but not in England's colonies.

By the time Samuel's conscience had become aroused to the evils of slavery, it was too late to change his business. His growing family depended on it. But he could fight the evil and did. Anti-slavery leaders often came to the house, and Elizabeth's ears rang with tales of cruel masters and cowering slaves in Jamaica and other British colonies. For a while she and the other children gave up using sugar, probably making Papa feel worse rather than better.

He was concerned about other evils than slavery. Most of the people of Bristol were poor and almost as much slaves as the blacks of Jamaica. Children were forced to work at the age of six from early morning till late at night. Six hundred paupers were confined in the city's poorhouse, with fifty-eight girls sleeping in ten beds and seventy boys in eighteen. Samuel was a Whig in politics, and the family was overjoyed when at last the Whigs came to power, and a Reform Bill was passed by the House of Commons. But it was defeated by the upper House of Lords, and the hopes of the poor were dashed. There were rumors of riots in other parts of the country. Though Papa sympathized with the poor, he believed justice should be won through law, not violence.

"We won't have trouble here," he said confidently. "Our people aren't that sort."

He was wrong. The family lived outside Bristol at a summer house during the hot weather, but twice a week the three girls rode with Papa into town for their lessons. One day in October, 1830, they found the tollgatherer at the city gate very excited.

"Better not go any farther." he told them. "The tax collector's here, and all h____ has broken loose!"

"But I must go. My house! My business!" Then

Papa hesitated. "I don't want you girls to be in danger. Perhaps I'd better take you back."

"No, no!" they insisted. "We're not afraid."

How they reached the house none of them could have told. Familiar lanes were deserted. Once, when they came to a street crowded with people, Papa wheeled the pony down another, but not before Elizabeth had caught a glimpse of some of the faces! They looked savage, like wild animals.

Papa herded them into the house, ordered them sternly not to leave it. Elizabeth threw her arms around him, begging him to stay where it was safe.

"Sorry, I can't, little Bessie. I must see what can be done. This madness must be stopped."

When he had gone, it was Elizabeth, not Anna, the oldest, who took charge while Marianne wept in a corner by the dining room fire. Anna rushed about pulling all the curtains. Calmly Elizabeth pulled them open. William White, one of Papa's most loyal workers, arrived, pale and trembling.

"Terrible," he moaned, "Whole town gone wild—tax collector's carriage pelted with stones!"

Elizabeth crouched by an open window, sick with worry for Papa. She wished desperately she were a boy, so she could rush out and find him. All day the noise continued. As dusk fell, it became louder—marching feet, yells, screams.

It was two in the morning when Papa returned, face gray with anxiety and weariness. Quiet had been restored. The worst seemed to be over. But he was wrong. Elizabeth woke to the sound of more shouts and running feet. Papa had gone. It was a day of terror. She crouched for hours at the upstairs window, Anna often by her side, their cold hands locked.

"Bessie, what shall we do?"

Elizabeth tried to be calm, reassuring. It was a queer feeling, knowing herself to be stronger than clever, fifteen-year-old Anna! She felt a hardness inside her, and a satisfaction which even drove out fear. She had lain on hard floors at night, thinking toughness was a thing of the body, when all the time it was something inside of you!

The whole city seemed to be in flames. The rioters were burning the Mansion House, the prisons where debtors were herded together in filthy cells, and the bishop's palace. Elizabeth understood why. It wasn't fair, they felt, that the bishop and magistrates should get high salaries when the people were starving. Then came the churches, the cathedral, and the Church of St. Mary Redcliffe. It was so beautiful, thought Elizabeth, even though Papa, being a Dissenter, hated everything connected with the Church of England!

At dusk rain fell in torrents, but it only seemed to make the fires burn harder. When Elizabeth heard Papa's voice, she rushed down the stairs. One of his friends was with him, and told her what had happened.

"You should have seen your father, child. He stood there in the doorway of the church of St. Mary Redcliffe and stretched his arms across! He faced that howling mob and made them listen. It was like arguing with a pack of wolves, but, by heaven, they turned around and went away. Nobody else could have done it. They knew he was on the side of the poor. They trusted him. And he helped save the cathedral; put out some of the fires with his own hands!"

"I did no more than others," said Papa.

Elizabeth stared at him with admiration. He was

a Dissenter, yet he had risked his life for those churches whose ways he so hated. Why? Because—her child mind fumbled—because he wanted other people to be as free as he was, to believe what they wanted to? She wished she were grownup, and a man, so she could have stood beside him!

3

JOURNEY TOWARD FREEDOM

To Elizabeth's surprise Papa did not seem to blame the rioters.

"Poor people," he sighed. "They thought it was going to bring peace and plenty. Instead, the same taxes and starvation wages."

Papa had been badly shaken by the riots. In fact, during the following winter, he seemed to become a different person—sober, almost sad.

Elizabeth would always remember this winter of her tenth year as the time when she stopped being a child. For the first time uncertainty and fear had entered her life. Wherever they went on their daily walks the scars were there: charred beams, blackened stones, vacant windows. Even the billowing sails of the ships coming into Bristol harbor had a frightening look. They might well be bearers of the deadly cholera, which had been creeping westward across Europe. Early in February, the month she was eleven, it struck London. Soon it hit Manchester, still nearer, where a whole family was swept away in a single day.

But it was the change in Papa which disturbed her most. She knew vaguely that he had suffered money failures, and that the sugar business had

not been prospering, but she could learn no
details. Even eight-year-old Sam seemed to know
more than she.

"It's business trouble," he dismissed her questions loftily. "Women are not supposed to worry
their heads about such things."

Then suddenly the blow fell. Two of the great
sugar importers' houses failed, and all Bristol
knew that Papa had been a heavy loser. Yet he
seemed more relieved than dismayed. He called
the family together in the dining room. With a
bounding heart Elizabeth saw that his stooped
shoulders were straight again, the glint back in his
blue-gray eyes.

"How would you like to go to America?" he
asked.

"You— you don't mean— not— not—leave—
England?" gasped Mamma. Aunt Bar grunted.
Aunt Ann reached for her smelling salts. Aunt
Lucy looked ready to faint. Aunt Mary nervously
fingered the trimming on one of her balloon-like
sleeves. Anna's cheeks reddened with annoyance.
Marianne looked sick. The two boys gave whoops
of excitement. Only Elizabeth, eyes fixed on
Papa's face, showed nothing of her tumult of
emotion.

Papa strode about the room while he talked. His
eyes glowed. He looked as young and enthusiastic
as eight-year-old Sam. In America, he told them, a
man could turn failure into quick success. The
boys would not be kept out of schools because
their father was a Dissenter. Perhaps he could
grow sugar beets, so he would no longer have to
depend on slave labor. It would be a new world of
freedom.

His Bristol friends were as shocked as some of
his family. He must not be allowed to go. They

promised to furnish him with any amount of money he needed, as a loan, for any number of years, at an interest of only 1½ percent. Papa thanked them but refused.

"If only he had been willing!" mourned Mamma. "Why—why isn't he ever able to let anybody help him?"

"Pride," replied Aunt Mary. "He's always been like that."

"But it would have been so easy! He didn't have to ask. They offered."

"I know. They really want him to stay. And if he did, I don't think there's any doubt that he would be elected mayor."

"I don't care about that." Mamma was weeping quietly. "All that matters is our having to leave everything we know and love and go across that terrible ocean to find heaven knows what."

"Does brother Samuel know how you feel?" demanded Aunt Mary.

Mamma looked shocked and hastily wiped her eyes. "Of course not. It's a wife's duty to follow her husband's wishes without complaint. Don't you dare tell him!"

In the days that followed Elizabeth was as joyfully excited as her brothers Sam and Henry. Yet she understood how Mamma felt. A lifetime was being torn out by the roots. The house was turned into salesrooms for all the beautiful rosewood and mahogany furniture and silverware. But Mamma insisted on taking her wedding china. Elizabeth helped pack it, in long shavings, proud to be entrusted with such treasures. Lovingly she stroked the delicate porcelain with its pattern of pagodas, of fragile bridges, of pink, red, and blue long-tailed birds, and of gold bands and rectangles.

The silver and other small articles were all set out in the back parlor, with prices marked for each lot. Half the women of Bristol, it seemed, came to inspect and bargain.

"Look at them!" fumed Anna. "Pawing everything, trying to beat the prices down! And they call themselves our friends! Pigs, all of them. I'm almost glad we're going away."

One day in August, 1832, a great crowd of friends and relatives came to the Bristol docks to see them off.

"We're like John Cabot," exulted Elizabeth, remembering the famous explorer who had sailed from this same port nearly four hundred years before in search of new worlds.

They were all on board at last—Papa and Mamma, the seven children (another soon to come), Aunt Bar, Aunt Lucy, Aunt Mary, and the two house servants Harriet and Jane. Aunt Ann had bravely chosen to stay in Bristol and teach school.

Elizabeth wept as they sailed down the winding river past the familiar scenes of her childhood jaunts and picnics and entered a stormy ocean, homesick in spite of her excitement. But she soon had ills to nurse worse than homesickness. A dose of hot arrowroot jelly helped, but did not cure the terrible nausea, and she was more seasick than most of the others all through the voyage.

The seven weeks and four days on board ship were a nightmare for all of them. The stern cabins which Papa had thought himself so lucky to secure tossed ten times worse then those amidship, and the windows leaked with every wind that blew. The cabin where Anna and Elizabeth were quartered, with four others, had an iron pillar in the middle of it, proving to their horror to be the drain leading from the deck's roundhouse to the water below, and it leaked incessantly. Anna was outraged.

"Horrid, filthy, stinking hole!" she kept muttering.

Far from escaping the troubles of the Old World, they discovered that they were taking one of its worst curses with them. Cholera soon broke out among the steerage passengers, and several died during the voyage. But except for seasickness, the family remained in good health.

Refusing to yield to the terrible seasickness, Elizabeth staggered weakly about the deck in pursuit of her lively brothers. A good thing she could not know that this long hard journey was a forerunner of future adventures like it. For this was by no means the last long hard trek into the unknown that would tax all the strength she could muster, because she was years ahead of her time.

4

LAND OF FREEDOM?

New York at last! It was night when they reached the pier, too late to disembark. But Papa took Sam and Henry and walked to a bake shop, and bought fresh bread; welcome indeed after the long diet of hardtack and salt beef. The next day he hired some rooms at two respectable boarding-houses on Pearl Street, side by side, kept by two maiden ladies. Since no transportation was available, the family walked there, their baggage in wheelbarrows, making a rather impressive procession of seven tired adults and seven excited children.

The cholera had arrived in New York before them, and they found the streets almost empty. Those of the two hundred thousand inhabitants who had not fled to the country were barricaded behind blank shutters.

But the cholera passed, and the city sprang into life again. The cobbled streets flowed with traffic. Shutters, most of them painted a rather ugly green, were opened. Every evening people came out of their plain, colorless houses to huddle on a small place in front called the "stoop."

"Not even a bit of a garden," thought Elizabeth

disapprovingly. Almost every house in England had a garden of some kind.

New York! It was indeed a new world, strange, exciting, but disappointing. Elizabeth had never felt more alone. Anna and Marianne, seventeen and fifteen, were now women, lacing themselves into tight, spindle-waisted corsets, padding their balloon sleeves, and thinking only of dress and sighing for England.

"These rough, filthy streets!" Anna fussed. "Not an impressive building in the town except maybe the city hall and the Merchants' Exchange!"

They all felt stifled in the ugly sliver of a house Papa rented on Thompson Street, such a contrast after the spacious rooms and gardens in England. The maids the family had brought with them struggled up and down steep flights of stairs. They dealt with strange shopkeepers in foreign money, and strenuously carried drinking water from a wooden pump at the corner. They were soon tearfully saving for passage back to England.

Mamma did not complain, but two faint lines in her pretty forehead showed her anxiety. The ocean journey was followed by months of further torments. She gave birth soon after they arrived. A few of her babies had died, so she anxiously watched over the cradle to find out if this baby they named George Washington Blackwell would live. She worked to keep peace in a household of so many people cramped into a small space.

Still, the demands of living, she found, were much the same in one country as in another. A man needed the same clean clothes, the same hot food, the same encouragement. Shirts must be sewed, pinafores made, socks mended. And most sniffles still responded to her same time-honored remedies:

Wrap your head up in flannel down to your eyes,
Put your feet in hot water up to your thighs;
Take a half pint of rum, going to bed, as a dose,
With a candle tip end, well tallow your nose.

Elizabeth missed England, but she thought New York a pleasant Dutch town, with its comfortable frame houses and shady parks. However, she felt none of the childish exuberance of Sam and Henry, though she was as excited as they when Papa took them for a sleigh ride up Bloomingdale Road, later to be called Broadway. She slid on the ponds at Washington Parade Ground, which would become Washington Square.

Though she worried about Mamma, Papa was her greater concern. For he had not solved his problems by coming to America. He had made them worse. True, his business was prospering. He had a nice new sugar refining plant on Gold Street. But he had left England to free his business from the bonds of slavery. In England slavery had been as far away as Jamaica; here it was on his own doorstep.

"There are twenty-five thousand colored people in New York," he wrote friends in England. "The smallest hint of colored blood is detected by American prejudice. They are excluded from schools, churches, and charities."

Though he bought his sugarcane now from Cuba instead of Jamaica, there was no difference. The Cuban planters said frankly that they did not try to raise slaves. It was more profitable to work them out in seven years or so, and when they died to fill their places with fresh slaves from Africa. Papa's suggestions about raising sugar beets were discouraged. "Too difficult and expensive," his allies said. And when he protested to his business friends about the evils of slavery, they were shocked and violent.

"You're joking! We'd all be out of business if the blacks were free!"

"What are you trying to do? Drive us all to the poorhouse?"

"What are you, a fool? Look out, or you'll see that sugarhouse of yours go up in flames some night!"

But he found people who shared his passion. One night Elizabeth sat in their tiny parlor listening to William Lloyd Garrison tell of his struggle to arouse opposition to slavery. The shades to the windows had to be drawn, he had so many enemies. His eyes gleamed as he told about the crowds who had hung on his words in Boston and Providence, the black people who clustered about him and wept. At last Papa had found an anti-slavery passion to match his own.

"Amen," he agreed fervently as Garrison spoke of obeying voices from heaven.

Elizabeth choked with emotion. But looking about the room she saw that none of the rest of the family seemed stirred. Mamma's pretty smiling face was bent over her sewing, one ear cocked for a warning whimper from baby Washy. Aunt Lucy and Aunt Bar were mending. Aunt Mary seemed to be listening politely, but her eyes held a vacant look, as if she were planning her early morning trip to market. Her brothers and sisters were fidgeting. What was the matter with them? How could they think about groceries and bonnets and—yes, even babies, when a battle for freedom was waiting to be fought?

She felt a fierce pride in Papa. It took courage for him to join Garrison's Anti-Slavery Society. Most leading citizens were opposed to the movement. She was with him one day in 1834 when a man speaking in a building near their home called slavery a crime and slaveholders murderers. A mob gathered outside and pelted the windows with stones. Amid the crash of falling glass and the howls of the mob, Papa managed to get his family out and safely home. For three days all except Papa stayed locked in the house while the mob attacked the homes, churches, and persons of blacks and abolitionists.

Perhaps it was fear resulting from this horror that caused Papa to move his family to Long Island. But he never yielded to fear. One night he came home from an abolitionist meeting with his hair disheveled and all the buttons torn from his plum-colored coat.

"Please," begged Mamma, "oh, please don't go to one of those terrible meetings again!"

"It's this country," snapped Aunt Bar. "Savages, all of them! Such a thing couldn't have happened in England."

Elizabeth stared at her. Had Aunt Bar forgotten all about the Bristol riots?

Living on Long Island did not remove them from all danger. One day in the summer of 1834 a tightly closed carriage rolled up to the door. Papa was the first to descend, and after him came a man, a woman, and five children. The woman and children had been crying. The man looked pale. Elizabeth recognized Dr. Samuel Cox, minister of the church the family had often attended in New York. Papa rushed the Coxes into the house as if he were afraid someone would see them.

"Our friends will be staying with us for a while," he said.

Elizabeth helped Mamma serve tea to the guests while listening with horror to Papa's account of what had happened. On Sunday Dr. Cox had preached a sermon on tolerance, begging his people to remain sane and not yield to the racial hatred that was sweeping the city.

"Jesus himself," he had reminded them, "was an Oriental, not a Westerner. He probably had darker skin than ours."

Word had got around that he had said Jesus Christ was black. A mob had attacked the church, smashed its windows, and broken into the parsonage. Warned that he was in danger of being lynched, Cox had fled with his family in a carriage Papa had provided.

Elizabeth's first heroic enthusiasm was soon lessened by the extra work resulting from the addition of so many more people to an already bulging household. The mere serving of tea each afternoon was a caterer's headache. At night Sam and Henry had to sleep rolled in blankets on the hall floor, and the girls fared little better on quilts in the hot attic.

A little later the minister's brother, Dr. Abraham Cox, who was the Blackwell family physician, joined the exiles.

Elizabeth's admiration of the minister's boldness soon turned to contempt. Already regretting his attempt to change people's thinking, he walked about sighing deeply, overwhelmed with fear and despair. If she ever had the courage like him to oppose public opinion for some noble cause, she certainly wouldn't back down and be sorry, even if it killed her.

"Turncoat, coward!" she muttered under her breath.

She had more admiration for Dr. Abraham in spite of his occasional moodiness, bad temper, and stubbornness.

"Let the mob come! We'll be ready for them!" he announced to the world at large. So he spent his time practicing pistol shooting behind the barn, his zeal greatly exceeding his skill, for several of the bullets landed in the back of the family carriage.

Even though they were pleased to protect the guests, the whole family breathed a sigh of relief when Dr. Cox, venturing into the city after ten days, decided it was safe to move his family back into the parsonage.

5

WESTWARD, HO!

The Blackwells did not remain on Long Island. Papa soon found a house across the Hudson River in Paulus Hook, later known as Jersey City. It was a big house set high on a hill above the river, with clean air, woods and fields close by, and one of the most exciting panoramas in the world to look at. Elizabeth loved to watch the flow of life on the Hudson—lofty frigates, merchantmen with strange flags, yachts with colored sails, ferryboats, and the skyline of New York in the background.

But she saw tragedy, too. One December night in 1835, they heard the clanging of fire bells across the river. Hurrying to the porch, they gasped. It looked as if the whole city were in flames.

"The sugarhouses!" Papa cried. He pulled on warm clothes and rushed to the ferry. Elizabeth stared with horror at the fire. It was like looking into the mouth of a volcano. It was hours before the flames began to subside, days before the billows of reddened smoke faded into gray.

After three days of terrified waiting Papa returned, pale and gaunt, clothes stiff with soot and dirt. The sugarhouses were untouched, but forty blocks of the city had been burned. Thousands were homeless and destitute.

That loss was followed by a bitter cold winter. Elizabeth often slept with a featherbed over her, as well as underneath. When Sam went to the city to buy her a present for her fourteenth birthday, the second of February, he was unable to get back because the river was filled with ice.

Spring came, and from a distance the remains of the fire's destruction seemed to have disappeared. Elizabeth began attending a school in New York. She was also taking private music and French lessons. She loved to study. Only one subject was distasteful—physiology. Anything connected with the body filled her with disgust. One day her professor, trying to interest the class in the wonderful structure of the body, brought the eye of a bull to the classroom. Elizabeth took one horrified glance at it and fled. For days she could hardly think of the incident without retching. She despised herself for this weakness.

She had always felt impatient with sickness of any kind. When in May she and Emily and Howie all came down with fever, she felt more angry and ashamed than miserable. One day, racked with chills, she had to leave school early, but she did not go home. Instead, she walked for miles into the country, head swimming, body shaking, and perspiring.

"I'll walk it off, I will, I will!" she said between clenched teeth. When she found she couldn't, she went home and shut herself into a dark room, locking the door and refusing to come out or let anybody in until the worst of the fever was over.

She was not popular and merry, like Marianne. All the sparkle seemed locked inside her. She took a fierce pride in her physical strength. Her small body was strong as steel, even though she was only a bit over five feet in height. More than once she settled arguments with one of her brothers by picking up her opponent and carrying him about the house until he was worn out with laughter and stopped arguing.

Physical prowess was satisfying, especially to a female, but it did little to relieve her frustrations. She was bursting with energy, and there were so few important things a woman could do! But into one activity she could pour all her fervor—the struggle against slavery. At one meeting of the Anti-Slavery Society, where Sarah and Angelina Grimké, daughters of slaveholders, spoke against slavery, more than three hundred women came.

One thrilling day Sam brought home a runaway slave girl who had taken refuge with friends. Afraid that her master had tracked her there, she desperately needed another shelter. She stayed with the Blackwells several weeks until Papa managed to get her on a ship to England.

Papa was becoming more silent and gloomy. Things had gone wrong with his business—in fact, with all businesses. It was 1837, a year of panic all over America. Suddenly the family was poor. Without a servant, the girls took turns doing the housework. Elizabeth dreaded the weeks when her turn came. In September it came more often. Anna went to teach music in a Vermont girls' seminary. Marianne also took a position teaching in a girls' boarding school.

Though finances sank to new lows, the family celebrated the Christmas holidays as usual. Sam and Elizabeth helped pick and weigh and wash and grate raisins, currants, and nutmegs for Mamma's famous Christmas puddings. When the day came they danced, played games, and had toast and cider for supper. They exchanged small presents. Three days later they managed to scrape up enough money to help a runaway slave on his journey to Canada.

To the family's dismay Papa began talking again about sugar beets, and about the wonderful opportunities out in the West.

"They say there are no sugar refineries beyond the mountains," he mused aloud, eyes once more gleaming. "Out there a man could be free, start all over, raise beets, get away from dependence on slavery!"

Elizabeth's heart sank. He sounded exactly the way he had back in England, before moving to America. But she was glad of anything that could bring back that smile to his lips and a gleam to his eyes.

Papa went west on a scouting trip and returned with a glowing description of a city named Cincinnati. They were to move there, he told them, and he was his old jolly self. He made fun of Jersey trees, which looked like dwarves beside the ones in Ohio. Cincinnati was the flourishing Rome of the West, with its seven hills and its glistening river.

Elizabeth knew what Anna would have said. "He's running away again, just as he did from England. Look at the money the sugar men are making now in Bristol, and will probably be making again in New York!"

But Elizabeth did not care. The glint in Papa's eyes, the spring in his step, silenced all her doubts. As soon as most of the household goods were sold at auction, they left by train for Ohio.

The journey was almost as long and hard as the one crossing the ocean. The first part, by railroad from Philadelphia, was comfortable enough, but when they reached the boat, which was to take them through the Pennsylvania Canal, the hardships started.

"Fitted up in a very superior manner," the advertisements had stated of the canal boat. Elizabeth and her mother and sisters were crowded into a room four by six yards, crammed with other women and roaring children. Already sixteen berths and most of the floor were occupied. They would have to spend three nights here, and the days on deck were almost as uncomfortable. Elizabeth was glad her aunts had remained in New York to run a millinery shop. Elizabeth was also glad Anna was not here with her tart tongue, or Marianne with her sickly tendencies. She could not bear to have Papa's enjoyment in his new venture spoiled by family worries.

After the canal came the strange journey over the Alleghenies in horse-drawn cars on what was called the Portage Railroad. At the foot of a slope the horses were unhitched and the cars fastened to a rope. A stationary steam engine at the head of the slope then moved the cars majestically up the steep incline. At a level place the horses were again attached until they reached the next slope.

They arrived at the top of the mountains about ten at night in a blinding snowstorm, and spent the night in a hotel. The storm was still raging when they started down the mountains the next morning. At Johnstown they returned to the canal boat.

Elizabeth's spirits were soon soaring again. Spring was in the air. The sun was bright, and flowers were blooming. She was able to walk with Papa for two or three miles along the canal bank. About twelve miles from Pittsburgh they anchored among a half dozen other canal boats, with only a field separating them from the Allegheny River.

It was one in the morning when Elizabeth finally heard the shout, "Steamboat coming!" The family struggled through a dense fog, trying to reach the boat before the best places were taken. But the berths in the women's cabin were already full. Elizabeth managed to find places for Mamma and the youngest children to lie down, but she and her sisters, Emily and Ellen, spent the night huddled against a wall. She could not forget how utterly tired Papa had looked after struggling with their heavy baggage.

But in spite of weariness, he set off at once when they arrived at Pittsburgh to arrange passage for Cincinnati. The *Tribune* turned out to be a colorful and jaunty boat. Fresh frocks emerged from the tin boxes. Mamma's face settled into its usual serenity, and Papa put on his new silk waistcoat. Most of the passengers were young and boisterous.

"I don't like the way some of those young men pay attention to our Emily and Ellen," worried Mamma.

Elizabeth regarded her younger sisters with sudden awareness—Emily was very pretty and poised at twelve; Ellen was ten, gay, and sparkling. No wonder the young men found their company stimulating while she could walk the deck without more than the respectful raising of a hat!

She fled to the mirror in the cabin. The face under her sober bonnet was delicate, eyes blue-gray and very clear, and the soft blond hair fell in neat coils over her ears. Still, she was colorless, that was the trouble, all pale and strawlike. But inside she was not at all colorless. Inside she felt power, like the power in the big engines that had pulled them over the mountains. Sometimes she felt that if she couldn't let it out, use her power in doing something important and worthwhile, she would burst.

They reached Cincinnati at last, after nine days' journey. Elizabeth's heart bounded. The city was beautiful, just as Papa had said. Its buildings clung to the sides of the encircling hills like the tiers of a great amphitheater. Even the mysterious backdrop of Kentucky slave country just across the river was part of the drama. On a stage like this, almost anything could happen!

6

A WOMAN COULD TEACH

They had lived in the big square stone house on Third Street in Cincinnati only since August 6, 1838, less than a month. Papa had not been well for months before that. There had been fainting spells, and after hiring a sugarhouse on the edge of the Ohio, he had had little energy to get the business started. But three days ago he had become very sick. All the medicines the doctors used—calomel, arrowroot, laudanum, brandy— had done little good.

Papa was dying! The family had stood around his bed all night listening to his harsh breathing, trying to ease his terrible fever with constant fanning. Though she was almost fainting from weariness, Elizabeth did not leave his side.

In the morning papa seemed to realize how sick he was.

"I've been an unworthy Christian," Elizabeth heard him whisper as she sat fanning him. "But I love God. He is my rock, my fortress, my deliverer." Presently his eyes opened and looked at her with their usual affection. "I beg you, try to get a little rest, my dear child." They were the last words she was to hear him speak to her.

A little later she came back into the room with a

cup of broth, to find Mamma kneeling beside his bed, his arms around her. He was saying in a painfully low voice, "Dear love, sorry—no money to leave you—"

"Please don't let that trouble you. Don't be anxious, my husband."

Elizabeth had just fled back to the kitchen when her mother called. "Elizabeth! Come quickly!" Heart beating wildly, she sped back to the room. "Papa thought it was you beside him," said Mamma in a calm voice. "He wants you to read the story of the annunciation in the Bible."

Elizabeth hurried to get the Bible, praying that she could read without her voice breaking. But he had sunk into a doze, and she tiptoed away.

That evening the whole family knelt by the bed and prayed silently. At about ten o'clock the doctor came. He looked at Papa and shook his head. It was all over.

Horrified, Elizabeth put her hand to Papa's mouth. Never would she forget the shock of finding there was no breath. But there was relief, too. Now they could weep without restraint.

Suddenly Elizabeth found herself the virtual head of the family. Mamma was like a small boat without its captain, rudder, and compass; the two older boys were in a state of shock. She sent letters to Anna and Marianne in the East, to the family in England. She arranged the parlor where Papa was laid out, she tried to explain the mystery of death to little Washy. Only after the funeral, in the sanctuary of her own room, did she find time again to weep.

But Elizabeth rose at dawn the next day, and laced herself into her tight stays like a soldier armoring for battle. She prepared to face the responsibility of a big family of six children, a year's lease to pay, rent due for the sugar refinery, doctors' and the undertaker's bills, and a frightening number of other debts. She soon discovered that she had exactly twenty dollars. She braced herself to face the future. Papa's debts must be paid.

Already she had a few music pupils. The second day after the funeral she taught them as usual. Sam and Harry announced vaguely that they would get jobs. Sam, slight of stature at fourteen, snapped quickly into manhood. Harry at thirteen was more jaunty. To Elizabeth's surprise her sister Emily made sensible suggestions and quietly shared tasks that must have been sheer drudgery for a twelve-year-old.

But it was Mamma who surprised her most. She burst into unexpected vigor. One day she called the family together. Though her voice was as gentle as ever, it held a new note of authority.

"We must use all our wits and energies to survive," she told them. "Elizabeth has suggested that we start a school, even before Anna and Marianne join us to help. We must have circulars printed and—" She looked suddenly frightened, but then her head lifted. "I shall go from house to house with them. Now let us kneel and ask God's help."

Yes, thought Elizabeth. There were few things a woman was permitted to do to earn money, that is, if she wanted to remain a *lady*. But *she could teach*. It was an occupation considered both respectable and proper for a female.

The circulars were printed, and Mamma went out to find pupils. Sam secured a job as a bookkeeper for the clerk of the superior court, and Harry got one as an errand boy. Elizabeth and Emily turned the big parlors into schoolrooms, and prepared bedrooms for boarding pupils.

The school opened, and ten days later, to Elizabeth's vast relief, Anna and Marianne arrived. Marianne, who now insisted on being called Marian, was prettier than ever, though she had developed a languid manner suggesting either a new sophistication or chronic invalidism.

But it was Anna who had really changed. Her clothes had incredibly tight waistlines and billowing skirts over heavily quilted petticoats, and she wore woolen shoes trimmed with pleated frills. Her world had expanded in New England. She had lived in the shadows of important men like Ralph Waldo Emerson, Horace Mann, and John Greenleaf Whittier.

But Anna was pleasantly surprised by Cincinnati, by its substantial brick houses, its clean wide streets. She was impressed by the friends the family had made, especially the Lyman Beechers. One of Lyman's sons was Henry Ward Beecher, who was to become the most popular preacher in America. Lyman's daughter Harriet, later to write *Uncle Tom's Cabin,* was married to Dr. Calvin Stowe, a professor in the theological seminary nearby. Mrs. Stowe was the mother of young twins and very busy, though she was already selling stories.

Elizabeth hated teaching, and her diary bristled with bursts of revolt:

Oct. 20—Oh, for a lodge in some vast wilderness, far away from children!

March 8—Friday. By the time school was over I was almost distracted. I really think if anyone came and proposed to me, I should have accepted without hesitation.

She did not even have her sisters' recourse to sickness as a reprieve from school. Anna, as well as Marian, was constantly being dosed for some ailment or other. Elizabeth was healthy. Still contemptuous of weakness, she accepted her role of nurse with less than sympathy. Her strength was as much of mind as of body.

Mamma was a good teacher, but inclined to be sweet, not firm. When the children became too boisterous, she would call to Elizabeth, who would come in and walk about, not saying a word. Somehow just looking at her, so straight and dignified, the most rebellious pupils would become as quiet as mice. Little did they know she was so terrified of them she quaked inside!

Now for the first time she was discovering the hardships of being female. For the boys, though only in their teens and with far less education, were able to earn twice as much as their sisters. And what occupations were open to a woman? Oh, yes, she could teach. She could sew, she could keep house for a married relative, or, like the aunts in England, she could live as a dependent on some member of her family. If she belonged to the lower classes, she could work in a mill with a pittance of pay and under unbelievably vile conditions.

Few husbands and fathers, she learned anew, were like Samuel Blackwell. Legally the wife was a slave of her husband. She had no separate existence apart from him. In most states a married woman's earnings belonged wholly to her husband. She could not hold property in her own name or make a will or contract.

"At least," Elizabeth told herself with grim satisfaction, "as long as I'm a spinster, unmarried, I can call what pittance I'm able to earn my own."

Papa had certainly been different, too, in believing women should have an equal education with men. Politicians, clergymen, and professional leaders were outspoken in denouncing equal education for women.

But, Elizabeth consoled herself, progress *was* being made. There was Emma Willard's Female Seminary in Troy, New York—the first endowed school for the education of girls. Miss Willard had even dared to introduce the subject of physiology, though, at the mothers' insistence the modesty of their daughters had been preserved by pasting heavy paper over pictures in the textbooks that showed any part of the human body. Then there was Oberlin Collegiate Institute in Ohio, the first college to open its doors to all regardless of race, color, or sex.

Misfortune came. The country in 1841 was in a financial crisis. The number of pupils decreased. Since the school was so small Anna went off to teach music in Dayton, Ohio. Family resources sank to a new low. For a time they could not afford fuel, even though they had moved to a smaller house. Without the paying guests they took on, they would have been desperate.

Marian's ill health made her undependable, and Mamma had been brought up to be a "lady," not a household manager. Elizabeth had to shoulder more and more responsibilities. After a twelve-hour day of teaching, marketing, and keeping the boarders decently warmed and fed, she should have been tired enough to fall into bed. Instead she went to lectures and church and anti-slavery meetings.

Perhaps because she felt herself to be a sort of prisoner, slavery became a burning issue for her more than ever before. She envied Sam when he went with some eighteen other men to Covington, Kentucky, as witness in a case seeking freedom for two black girls who were kidnapped in Ohio.

The Kentucky "slave country" across the Ohio River held a terrible fascination for her. The pretty little towns of Newport and Covington looked beautiful, yet mysterious and sinister.

To her dismay, in 1844 she was offered a position as teacher in a school in Henderson, Kentucky. She could not refuse; their school had closed, and she had become just another mouth for the family to feed. Sam and Harry both had good jobs, and Emily, grave and adult at seventeen, was as capable as Elizabeth of running the household. Little Washy was as tall as she and already working part-time jobs.

No, she was no longer needed at home. She was twenty-three years old, an age when most women were married and having children. Horrified, she looked forward to her probable future—earning a little by giving music lessons, or pursuing the ladylike task of helping to run some other women's household. No she would not be like her aunts! Spinster, perhaps. Dependent, no. She would go to Kentucky.

When the jaunty little steamer *Chieftain* was four days and a hundred miles from Cincinnati, she became panic-stricken. The little towns along the river looked more and more dingy. At last the boat swung toward the bank.

"Henderson!" shouted the pilot. Elizabeth saw only three dirty old frame buildings, and a steep mud bank with some blacks and unprepossessing looking whites gathered at its foot. The boat touched. She stumbled uncertainly, and a man came forward and presented his arm.

"Howdy, miss. I'm Dr. Wilson." He gestured curtly to one of the blacks. "You there, boy, tote up her baggage." Dr. Wilson was the man who had written to and hired her.

She struggled after him up the bank. They passed through the little village, and stopped at a substantial brick house. Her hostess, a tall, graceful, sleepy-eyed girl, took her to a small, high-ceilinged bedroom. She was to occupy it with three sisters. But to her relief all, as well as the mother, were clean, pleasant and attractive. In fact, their chief fault was a friendliness which made impossible the privacy she loved. She went downstairs again to Dr. Wilson.

"I would like to begin teaching," she said, "on Monday morning."

When she took her seat in front of a class of fourteen girls, she found they were quiet and pleasant, much gentler than the children she had taught in Cincinnati. After school she taught music and French to private pupils, which meant that three days a week she taught for ten hours. She wished that on the other days she had as much to do. She did not find a single person with whom she could enjoy an interesting conversation.

Her hatred of slavery grew, even though she knew she was seeing it only in its mildest form, for the Kentuckians prided themselves on the happy lot of their slaves.

"Plenty to eat, a roof over their heads. Better off than the poor in your England!"

But they aren't free! she wanted to retort. *How would you like to be owned like a horse or cow?* But she dared not speak her mind.

One day she was sitting with her hostess on the broad shaded veranda when the oldest daughter, tall and graceful in her floating summer finery, came out on her way to church. Just at that moment a shabby, black slave came toward the veranda. He stood hesitantly, eyes pleading. "Please, ma'am, could I have——clean shirt for Sunday?"

His mistress' placid face creased with annoyance. "Of course you can't have a clean shirt. You had one last week. And you know better than to come to the front door." Meekly he went away.

But it was another incident that she would remember as long as she lived.

One evening she went to visit at the home of one of her pupils. Refreshments were served by a small, black girl with huge dark eyes and teeth even whiter than Harry's. The tray was much too big for her, and she slopped the tea. The hostess reprimanded her sharply.

"You'd think," she apologized, "as how that Lily could do things decent by this time. Here we've owned her since she was scarce bigger'n a grasshopper."

Elizabeth choked on her tea. She felt the hot blood rushing to her cheeks.

"Is anything the matter, miss?" inquired the hostess anxiously.

"No—no, I–I'm just a bit warm, I guess. The fire is really hot."

"Lily!" The gentle voice turned harsh. "Stand between teacher and the fire."

"Oh— no— please! I'm really all right."

But her protests were of no avail. She had to sit, talking pleasantly, while the slave child, barefoot and scantily clad, made a living firescreen of her puny, unprotected body. The heat must have been blistering. It did not help to know that her hostess had only wanted to be kind and hospitable.

Elizabeth could not stand such injustice for long. At the end of her first term she left Henderson and went back to Cincinnati.

7

"WHY DON'T YOU BECOME A DOCTOR?"

Home again! At first it seemed like perfect freedom. The family had moved to the suburb of Walnut Hills, near Lyman Beecher's family. Elizabeth attended meetings of the Anti-Slavery Society and sewed garments for fugitive slaves. And she fell in love.

The man was highly cultured and educated, and Elizabeth, feeling herself totally unattractive, was shy to the point of torture in his presence. But in the autumn when he began to show an unmistakable interest in her, she blossomed like an opening bud. It was the happiest time she had ever known. The air seemed more exhilarating, and the stars more blazing bright. One evening when he came to call he brought a bouquet of late blooms, and she nursed it for days in a vase, then laid the drying wisps in her bureau drawer.

Then, like the bouquet, autumn faded, and with it the radiance of romance. One day she shared with him some passages from a book she had been reading by the French writer, Fourier. She did not expect him to agree with its controversial theories. She wasn't sure she did herself. But his reaction was shocking.

"Come now, you shouldn't bother that pretty

little head about theories no woman can understand. Leave the reforming of the world to men.
It's our responsibility to run it."

She stared at him, unable to speak. She could
have stood criticism, welcomed it, but—*patronizing*
her because she was a woman!

"Let me bring you some books, poetry, nice
little essays, the sort of things a woman should
read, something that—"

That doesn't require any real thinking, she finished
for him silently. "Yes, please do," she said politely.

That night she thrust the wilted blossoms into a
paper bag and threw it into the wastebasket. Then
she seized a black, wool cape from the hall rack,
fled from the house, and began walking. But the
cold air stirred her restlessness instead of calming
it. What would she be ten years from now? A
spinster with nothing more worthwhile to do than
go to teas and meetings? Worse yet, a meek wife
with no real life apart from her husband's? Life
seemed to be rushing past her. If only she had
some goal with an all-consuming purpose!

Was it just coincidence that a few days later she
called on a close friend, Mary Donaldson? She had
dreaded the visit with her usual dislike of sickness
and weakness, for Mary was dying of an incurable
disease.

"My dear, how good of you to come!" Mary
said, her eyes as lively as ever. "See, I've had my
bed moved near the window, but I can't see half as
much as I'd like to. Tell me everything that's been
happening."

Elizabeth relaxed. They talked pleasantly of
local events, people they knew. Finally, fearing
she was tiring Mary, Elizabeth rose to leave; but a
thin hand reached out to hold her back.

"Wait, dear. For some time I've wanted to say something to you."

Reluctantly Elizabeth sat down again.

Mary's eyes held a fevered intensity. "It's a terrible thing, Elizabeth, to die a slow death like this, but there's one thing that would have made the suffering so much easier for me. If— if only I didn't have to be examined and treated by a *man!*" Elizabeth felt Mary's fingers tighten. "You're young and strong, my dear. You have a keen mind and like to study. Why don't you try to become a doctor?"

"A— doctor?" echoed Elizabeth faintly.

"Yes. Please, my dear, promise you will at least think about it?"

Mary's eyes were steady and insistent. They demanded an answer.

"I— I promise," Elizabeth said finally.

Snowflakes brushed her cheeks as she climbed the hill toward home. The click of her heels on the hard ground took on a queer rhythm. Doc - tor . . . Doc - tor, they seemed to pound. What a preposterous idea! The very word brought unpleasant memories— that staring bull's eye; her father's beloved face, with flesh yellowed, eyes glazed; endless spooning of medicines between sick lips. Anyway, it was impossible. Whoever heard of a woman doctor?

But the idea kept rearing its head like a jack-in-a-box. *You wanted a challenge, a consuming purpose in life.* What could be more so?

Most of all it pursued her as she fled from painful meetings with the man she still felt attracted to. She would not marry him, yet could not forget him. But if she had some other all-consuming goal . . . Why not put such an impassable barrier between them?

She could think of a dozen reasons. She was twenty-four, too old to start years of training. She had no money. She hated sickness. And it was the worst possible career for a woman to choose. Why then did the words of a dying woman persist in challenging her against all reason? "My dear, *why don't you become a doctor?*"

One day she startled her mother by a blunt question. "Mamma, tell me what it's like to bear children."

Her mother blushed. It was a subject no lady of the mid-eighteen hundreds would think of discussing. "Why, I— I—"

Elizabeth persisted. "You've had doctors for your childbearing and other sicknesses. Would it have made your suffering any easier to bear if you had had a good woman doctor?"

The shocked restraint was suddenly unloosed. "Oh— yes! You have no idea of the shame and embarrassment involved for a lady of delicate upbringing!"

Finally, outwardly calm but inwardly quaking, she dared to broach the subject to the family.

"What would you say if I told you that I am thinking of trying to become a doctor?"

Being Blackwells, her brothers and sisters were neither shocked nor surprised. Harry expressed immediate approval. Sam slowly nodded. "If you think it's the thing to do, sis, we'll all be behind you."

Marian said shrewdly, "But you hate taking care of sick people. A doctor should be sympathetic."

Elizabeth did not evade her accusing eyes. "I know. I've often been impatient with you. But— I do care about people."

She was glad Anna was not there. Elizabeth could imagine her tart, "What! Little Shy trying to break into a world no other woman has ever entered?"

It was her mother who surprised Elizabeth most. "I wish," she said, "that your father could be alive to see his Bessie show such courage!"

But the assurance of family was not enough. One day she went to see Harriet Beecher Stowe, who lived nearby. It was April, and all her senses were aware of the color and warmth. If ever there was a time to start a new and daring life, this was it.

But she saw at once that she had come at the wrong time. Harriet was scratching furiously on a sheet of paper. Her table was piled high with books, the floor littered with toys. A baby was asleep nearby. Though Harriet was cordial enough, Elizabeth felt her own enthusiasm fading.

Harriet put down her pen. "You're really serious about this, my dear?"

She might have been talking to one of her children caught in some foolhardy activity, like flying off the roof under an umbrella.

"Of course I'm serious!" Elizabeth said indignantly.

"Very well. Then of course I'll do what I can to help. Let me consult Mr. Stowe. He's much more practical than I."

Elizabeth walked home slowly, the luster gone out of the day. She waited impatiently for Mrs. Stowe to send word that she wanted to see her again. When word came, she could not travel the path fast enough.

"My dear, I have talked with Mr. Stowe about your plan. I hate to be discouraging, but— he seems to think it is entirely impracticable. Commendable, of course," she hastened to add, "but

53

we think there is too much prejudice. You would either have to crush it or be crushed by it."

Elizabeth went home. Things that were hard had always challenged her. She wrote asking advice from doctors whom the family had known, and letters began coming back. They were unanimous—the idea was impossible. But there was still Dr. Abraham Cox, the doctor they had known back in New York, to be heard from. He was no comformist. He had dared to speak out against slavery. She waited anxiously for his reply. When it came, she went upstairs, shut herself in her room, and opened it. Her heart was racing.

"The idea is a good and valuable one," he wrote kindly, "but it won't work. There is no way for a woman to obtain a medical education." However, he was glad to give her names of medical schools and tell her how she should apply.

The idea is a valuable one! Surely, thought Elizabeth, *if an idea is valuable, there must be some way to realize it*. Difficult? Yes, but she had never been afraid of difficulties. Suddenly words spoken to another woman, Queen Esther, in a long-ago age flashed into her mind. *Who knoweth whether thou art come to the kingdom for such a time as this?*

It was in that moment that she made up her mind. And no discouragement, no difficulty, no misfortune, would turn her from her purpose.

"I *will*—" she vowed stubbornly.

8

"I <u>WILL</u> BE A DOCTOR!"

Yes, she would become a doctor. But how to begin? First, she must have money. She would have to teach and lay up enough to see her through at least a few months of medical school.

Less than a week after she made her decision a letter came from Anna offering her a position as a teacher in Asheville, North Carolina. Dr. John Dickson, who was principal of the school, was a physician, and she would live in the Dicksons' house! A double blessing! Not only earning money, but living in a doctor's house! Surely he could give her a start in her medical studies! She wrote immediately, eagerly accepting the position.

Sam offered to drive her to Asheville, sacrificing nearly a month's work. The last night Elizabeth could not sleep. She rose at dawn and after tearful farewells they started out, Sam, Elizabeth, and fourteen-year-old Howie, in a borrowed carriage drawn by an old horse, Fanny. It was six o'clock on Monday morning, June 16, 1845.

"Rosinante," Sam called the plodding Fanny, after the horse in *Don Quixote*, one of the family's favorite stories. And it was an appropriate name, for the trip of nearly two weeks through Kentucky and the Virginia and Tennessee mountains was certainly quixotic, and unpredictable. It was full of discomfort, but also of pleasures. Elizabeth would never forget the view from the top of Cumberland Gap, where Virginia, Kentucky, and Tennessee lay spread beneath them in breathtaking beauty. When they arrived in Asheville on Friday, June 27, she felt both hope and exhilaration.

But the happy excitement fled when she retired to her strange new room in a strange new home on Sunday evening. The Dicksons were all she had hoped for, cultured and hospitable people. Her room was pleasant and airy. But her brothers had gone, cutting her last link with all the twenty-four years of her life. She stood at the open window staring out at the mountains that were barely visible in the starlight. Suddenly she was overwhelmed with doubt and terror. Was it all wrong, this determination to travel a path that no woman had ever dared to enter?

"Oh, God help me!" she cried silently.

She was suddenly conscious of a presence. Nothing visible, but somehow it flooded her with a brilliant light. The fear and doubt vanished. She *knew* that no matter how small her success might be, she was following that divine will which directs human progress.

Life at Asheville was pleasant. She liked her school. But there were many frustrations. Coming here to this part of the country where slavery prevailed, she had resolved to teach all the slaves possible to read and write.

"Sorry." Dr. Dickson said regretfully, for he was at heart an abolitionist. "It's against the law to teach them."

"You mean," Elizabeth was horrified, "no effort is made to teach—"

The principal smiled. "Only an occasional sermon."

But, he told her, it might be possible to start a small Sunday school. And she did. She found four women and one man willing to help. They divided the twenty-five scholars who turned up on the first day among them. Her group of four ranged in age from eight to twelve. Eagerly she faced them.

"Suppose we learn a Scripture verse," she said, smiling brightly. "Thou shalt love the Lord thy God with all thy heart . . ." The four voices repeated the verse, low and frightened at first, but gaining confidence. "This is the first and great commandment. And the second is like unto it. Thou shalt love thy neighbor . . ."

She stopped. Trying to teach those poor little children a religion, which their *owners* professed to follow while not even treating them like human beings, much less loving them as their neighbors, seemed absurd to Elizabeth at the moment. She looked around the room, staring at the one man and four women preaching to their slaves. She wanted to scream.

"Is— is anything the matter, mum?" asked a small pupil timidly.

"No. Nothing." Elizabeth smiled and went on quietly teaching.

She felt frustration, too, in her main purpose. Progress was so slow! Dr. Dickson was as helpful as possible. He even borrowed a human skeleton, so she could learn something about anatomy. One day she was introduced to dissection.

"Here's a specimen for you," said Miss Maria, one of the other teachers, with a hint of mischief. "It met its death from being shut up in my perfume box."

Elizabeth looked at the big beetle and felt sick.

But she knew there was no evading the challenge. Gingerly seizing the huge insect with a hairpin, she placed it on a piece of paper and took her mother-of-pearl penknife in her hand.

"It's dead," she told herself. "Nothing I do can hurt it."

But her fingers seemed paralyzed. How could she ever learn to be a doctor if she couldn't conquer her horror of handling dead things? A half hour had passed when, with quivering stomach but steady fingers, she lowered the knife, and with a sickening crunch cut off the creature's head. No brains, she noticed, with what she hoped was a proper medical student's reaction. Boldly she split it down the middle. Nothing but a little yellowish dust! So! She felt as if she had won a major battle. Never would she feel such squeamishness again.

That January Dr. Dickson decided to close his school and move to a free state. With this change Elizabeth was sure she'd become frustrated, but the change proved a blessing.

"I have written my brother in Charleston, South Carolina," he told her, "and he invites you to come and be a part of his household. Sam is a practicing doctor, and he can help you far better than I could. And he has promised to find you a teaching job."

Elizabeth was overjoyed. What an opportunity! It seemed almost too good to be true.

It was a journey not only from the country to the city, but from one world to another. There were beautiful palmettos, gray Spanish moss, and wild orange and live oak trees. They made January seem like April. The water-brimming rice fields were as blue as the sky. The great acres of cotton fields were bordered with belts of evergreen. She loved it.

And to her joy Dr. Samuel Dickson was as bold and adventurous as she. Not only did he find a position for her teaching music in a fashionable school, but he put his fine library and all his medical knowledge at her disposal. She studied his medical books, often far into the night, wrapped in a blanket. She pored over anatomy charts and specimens in his laboratory, and read a lot about medical history.

To her joy she found that there had been capable women healers in the past; not in America, but in other countries. In fact, once the art of healing had seemed to belong to women. The Hebrew midwives mentioned in the Bible may have been trained in Egyptian medical schools. There were female doctors in Greek and Roman history. Some of the early Christian Roman women devoted their lives to healing and established hospitals.

To her amazement she even found her own name in the history of female medicine. *Elizabeth Blackwell!* She could hardly believe her eyes. Her namesake had lived a century before, a Scotswoman who had studied with her doctor husband and practiced as a midwife. She also published a book on healing herbs. It was like finding a signpost on a strange road. She felt as if in choosing this career she was fulfilling a plan for her life set long before her birth. She was *meant* to become a doctor.

Only one time did she almost lose courage.

"It's time," said Dr. Sam, "that you read some books on surgery. That is," his eyes were kind but probing, "you do intend to become a surgeon?"

"Oh— oh, yes!"

"Then suppose you start with these." He gave her two books by Robert Liston, a London doctor, and one of the most skillful surgeons living at that time.

"Thank you."

Elizabeth took them, hoping her hands were not trembling, and fled to her room. They lay untouched for days. It was the hardest test she had yet faced. Here was no dead beetle to be slit with a knife, not even a human corpse to be somehow dismembered. It was living, quivering, human flesh.

She opened the books finally, with the same unhesitating precision that she had used to cut off the beetle's head, and entered the world of surgery. She had a vivid imagination. No actual visit to an operating room could have been more revealing. Scalpels slashed, blood spurted, flesh quivered. She dreamed of operating chairs that turned into torture racks, scalpels that became butchers' cleavers, and she woke with the screams of patients ringing in her ears.

By a strange coincidence during that same fall of 1846, something was happening in Boston that would change surgery for all time. Dr. John Warren, one of the country's most skillful surgeons, was about to perform an operation on a young man for a growth on his tongue.

"Gentlemen," he said to the young medical students who had come to watch, "a Boston dentist named Morton is coming at ten o'clock to try out a preparation that he says will free our patient from pain during his operation."

There was laughter from the students. Warren himself sounded disbelieving. Cut into a person without his feeling any pain? Unheard of! Impossible!

"Humbug!" someone shouted.

Dr. Warren put on an old black jacket, stiff with dried blood from many operations. As yet cleanliness was not considered necessary in preventing infection and disease. He assembled his tools, scalpel, forceps, and some glowing irons on a charcoal burner. Ten o'clock came. No Morton. The students laughed again. Warren had just taken his scalpel in hand when the door burst open, and a young man rushed in. He carried a glass globe connected to a tiny tube. Warren gestured toward the patient. The man placed the tube in the patient's mouth.

"Please breathe deeply," he said. The air filled with a strong sweetish odor. The patient's eyes closed. His head fell to one side.

"Your patient is ready, Doctor."
Warren stepped forward, raised his knife, and made a swift incision. The expected screams from the patient did not come. He proceeded to operate without a sound. When he had finished, he stood staring at the patient, who remained silent, quietly breathing. At last he looked around the room.

"Gentlemen," he said in an awed voice, "this is no humbug."

This discovery of ether as an anesthetic was reported in a Boston newspaper on November 18, 1846. It was almost the exact day when Elizabeth wrote her sister Marian, "My mind is fully made up. I am resolved to go through with the study of medicine."

But how? After a year in Charleston she had saved little money, for her small salary was just enough to live on. In February of 1847 she had her twenty-sixth birthday. She felt like a trapped bird beating its wings against a cage. But then came a letter from Dr. Warrington, a Quaker physician in Phildelphia, to whom she had written for advice.

"I beg thee to believe with me," he wrote kindly, "that if the project be of divine origin it will sooner or later be accomplished." He told her to visit him if she came to Philadelphia. Her spirits soared. She had written to many doctors, but this was the first time one had given her the slightest encouragement.

She went to Philadelphia in May, taking her month's pay. The rest of her savings had been put in a New York Bank. She also took a prized collection of bones given her by Dr. Sam, and a certificate stating the study she had completed under his teaching. And she certainly couldn't have gone without her determination, as tough and unbending as steel.

Dr. Warrington was as kind as his letter. But even more helpful were Dr. and Mrs. William Elder, Quakers with whom she secured lodging. She tried to be admitted to one of Philadelphia's four medical colleges, but with no success. Dr Warrington arranged for her to take anatomy lessons in a private school. She went to her first lesson fearful and trembling. Her thoughts were on the dead beetle and her horrifying dreams of screams and blood and scalpels.

"Suppose we start our lessons," said her teacher Dr. Allen, "with a study of the human wrist."

What followed was more than a lesson in anatomy. She felt as if she were joining God in his work of creation. The beauty of the tendons, the marvelous bone structure, the wonderful arrangement of veins and nerves and muscles! It was like seeing a miracle performed before her eyes. Instead of fear and distaste, she felt only wonder and admiration. Never again would she be horrified by the marvels of the human body.

But as she consulted other Philadelphia doctors, she felt first encouragement, then disappointment, amusement, hope, and finally despair. All agreed that it would be impossible for a woman to study medicine. Even Dr. Warrington became pessimistic.

"Elizabeth," he said to her finally, "it is no use trying. Thou canst not gain admission to these schools. If thou must continue in this undertaking, then thou must go to Paris and wear men's attire to gain the necessary knowledge."

No! Her whole being revolted. Not that she objected to going to Paris, but to gain her goal through deception? She had started on a crusade, to open the door of a noble profession to all women, not just herself. But— how?

Dr. Warrington helped her obtain a list of smaller medical schools in the northern states. She picked out a dozen and sent applications to all of them. Should she sign her name E. Blackwell, perhaps making them think she was a man, then, once admitted, browbeat them into keeping their pledge? No, again. That would be almost as deceitful as wearing men's clothes.

Twelve times she signed her name in her bold neat slanting script: Elizabeth Blackwell. Nothing but refusals. She tried more and more schools. Finally she had applied to twenty-nine different medical colleges. Waiting was torture. Time for the beginning of the winter session for classes drew near, came and passed. Must she wait another year? The suspense was torture.

Then suddenly she received a letter from a small college in Geneva in upper New York state. She was accepted! At last! She felt relief, gratitude, but not surprise. She had never believed failure possible.

Immediately she accepted the invitation, and on November 4, 1847, she started on her long trip to western New York state, arriving in the little town of Geneva on the evening of November 6. It was the beginning and the ending of a journey.

9

150 MEN AND ONE WOMAN

Fortunately Elizabeth had no idea that her acceptance by the Geneva Medical School was due to a mistake!

When the dean, Dr. Charles Lee, received a letter from Dr. Warrington recommending a Miss Blackwell as a student, he found himself in a quandary. Dr. Warrington was a reputable physician known to the staff. He heartily recommended the applicant as a good student, respectable, sincere in her desire to become a doctor. She had been refused by several medical colleges, but he thought Geneva more likely than others to be free from prejudice. True, the school had been founded on democratic principles. But—admit a woman! Impossible! Yet—what to do? After a long and painful consideration, Dr. Lee and the rest of the staff arrived at a happy solution.

"Gentlemen," he said to the assembled class of medical students, "I have here a letter containing the most extraordinary request ever made to the faculty." He read the letter. There was dead silence when he finished. "The faculty have decided—" The whole room seemed to be holding its breath, "decided to leave the matter in the hands of you gentlemen. If a single student objects to her admission, a negative reply will be returned. We shall wait for your answer."

He left, feeling that the problem was well solved. Of course there would be not one objection but many. Trust these somewhat rowdy students, many of them country boys from the surrounding rural area, to resent the intrusion of a troublesome female!

As soon as the door closed pandemonium broke loose. There were catcalls, hoots, and loud exclamations.

"Women doctors! How about men mothers?"

"I say it's a great idea!"

"What would we call her? Doctress? I'll bet she's six feet tall and has a mustache."

The class met that evening to discuss the problem. The meeting was hilarious. There were more exclamations.

"One lady to a hundred and fifty men! Imagine it!"

"You really think she could be called 'lady'?"

"I'd like to see her in dissection! What a lark!"

Stratton, the class president, had to pound the desk for at least five minutes to make himself heard. "Gentlemen! gentlemen!" Somehow he managed to impress on the group the serious nature of their decision. The fate of the Geneva medical classes might well rest upon it. If anybody wanted to speak for or against the admission, now was the time to address the floor.

One man rose, was recognized, and proceeded with mock sincerity. "There has been something lacking in our classrooms, delicacy, refinement, beauty, all the attributes of the fairer sex."

"Hear, hear! Bravo!" The speaker was acclaimed with vigor by the rambunctious crowd, their shouts resembling catcalls rather than applause.

They're going to put it through! thought Stephen Smith, one of the more serious students, in amazement. What a joke on the faculty! By heavens, they might be making history here tonight! Suppose a hundred years from now people looked back and remembered! He got up and made a short speech about the ideal of equality in education.

At last Stratton pounded the desk. "Gentlemen, I want you to understand that if you vote to admit this—this lady, you are pledging to conduct yourselves in her presence like gentlemen. Now—all those in favor?"

"Yea!" The class rose to its feet and a barrage of hats hit the ceiling.

"Opposed?"

"No." The word came from a timid voice in a corner.

There was a gasp of disbelief, then a dozen figures rushed toward the dissenter. There was a chorus of screams.

"Cuff him!" "Throw him downstairs!" "Say yea, you traitor!"

"Yea," he croaked. The vote was declared unanimous.

Most of the class left in a hilarious mood. What a joke, outwitting the faculty, and what a lark, having a woman in their midst! Only a few, like Stephen Smith, had more sober ideas. Did this female (he could not quite bring himself to say lady) know what she was getting herself into? One woman in a class of one hundred and fifty men, many of them rowdies? Heavens! What sort of woman was she? A Joan of Arc? An Amazon? He could hardly wait to find out.

Two weeks passed, and she had not arrived. It was a Monday morning. Another week of lectures, and bedlam had already started with more zest than usual, for Dr. Lee was late. Erasers were flying. At the windows overlooking a girls' normal school some students were bunched for glimpses of less timid females, peeping from behind their blinds.

Suddenly Dr. Lee entered, and the students rushed to their seats. Lee stopped before the tiers of benches, opened his mouth and closed it, as if he didn't know quite what to say.

"Gentlemen." His voice actually trembled. "I must inform you that the—the lady student has arrived." He opened the door. Not a sound could be heard as a woman entered and went to the lecture platform, where he placed a chair for her. "Gentlemen, Miss Elizabeth Blackwell."

Stephen Smith stared with the others. An Amazon? A Joan of Arc? This tiny creature, dressed in Quaker gray, eyes demurely downcast beneath a plain bonnet? This was no mannish freak, no bold crusader. She was a lady, refined, modest, even diffident. There was a firmness and determination about her, yes. But it would take more than firmness and determination to storm one of man's most jealously defended citadels. He felt sorrow for her—and admiration.

For the first time Dr. Lee was able to give his lecture in complete silence. The order in the classroom was uncanny. Elizabeth was the only person in the room taking notes.

At the end of her first day in medical school she felt almost as gloomy as the weather. Rain beat against her windows in Miss Waller's boarding-house as she threw another stick of wood in her small stove and huddled over it, chilled to the bone.

True, she had been allowed to attend all the lectures, and her teachers had loaned her notes for the ones she had missed. All, that is, except one. Dr. Webster, the professor of anatomy, had been absent, and his assistant had been unwilling to admit her to dissection without his permission. Dr. Webster, she had heard, was a queer duck. Suppose he refused to let her into his classes. She had to study anatomy and dissection to graduate. Suddenly she realized that one balky professor could jeopardize all her chances of success.

It had been hard to secure a room. She had called on at least a dozen landladies. The responses had been similar: "Sorry, rooms all taken." "No vacancy." "We cater to men only." Yet more than one window had displayed the sign, Room for Rent. Not until long afterward would she learn that many had been threatened with the loss of some of their best patrons if a female medical student were received.

But finally she had found the cheerful, motherly Miss Waller.

"A room? Of course, my dear. Any friend of Dr. Lee is welcome here. I have several empty. What sort would you like?"

"The smallest and cheapest, if you please."

It was small, certainly, up in the attic, but, hung with pictures she had brought and furnished with her personal belongings, it had seemed almost homelike. Until tonight.

On Elizabeth's second day rain and wind whipped her long skirts as she walked to the college. Then, because of a jolly fat anatomy professor, the day suddenly turned cheerful. How she had dreaded meeting him! But to her surprise, she found that he was a plump, little man who shook her hand warmly, and seemed to beam all over. Expecting to find a ferocious lion, she had found a purring pussycat.

"Just what we need around here," he beamed at her, "a lady pupil. Welcome, Miss Blackwell!"

"Thank you, Dr. Webster," she said gratefully.

"Now suppose you wait in the anteroom a minute. The lesson today concerns a most delicate operation, and—well, I just want to make sure the class is still on its good behavior."

She waited outside, breathless with anxiety. There was a sound of laughter, a round of applause, then the little man appeared, face beaming like a plump sun, and ushered her to a seat. The lecture proceeded quietly as had all the other classes. She could not know that until her coming serious students had found it hard to hear the lectures because of the prevailing rowdiness. At the end of the session she found Dr. Lee waiting outside, his face looking anxious.

"Everything went—smoothly, I hope?"

"Oh— yes, sir. And I am much impressed with the quality of teaching."

Dr. Webster came bustling toward them. He seemed bursting with merriment. "You attract too much attention, Miss Blackwell. There were many strangers present this afternoon. I shall have to guard against this."

Dean Lee's face brightened. Relief made him almost jovial. "Who knows?" He chuckled. "This step might prove a good advertisement for the college. It could certainly attract notice, and the college needs it right now."

Who did know, indeed? Certainly the dean could not have guessed that a faculty's cowardice and a student body's bravado would be the small college's chief claim to fame a century later!

The sun was shining when Elizabeth returned to her room. She wrote in her diary, "Attended the anatomy class—very clear—how superior to books! Oh, this is the way to learn! The class behaves well, and all the people seem kind."

No, not all of them. Of course her careful aloofness did not discourage the male students entirely. Once while a lecturer was giving a demonstration that a less objective woman might have found embarrassing, she felt something fall on her arm. Looking down, she saw a bit of folded paper, evidently a note, lying on the sleeve of her black dress. Some impertinence, of course. She felt every eye in the room upon her. She slowly lifted the note until it was in view of the whole room, and with a flick of her wrist let it fall to the floor. There was a round of applause, and such an action was never repeated.

"The attention I attract is a matter of perfect indifference," she wrote Marian. "They might be mummies for all I care. I believe the professors don't exactly know in what species of the human family to place me, and the students are a little bewildered."

At first she had not the least idea of the commotion she created in the town. When small boys stared at her as she walked from Miss Waller's to the college, she thought it was just childish curiosity. Until she heard whispers and mumbles accompanying the stares!

"Here she comes!"

"Come on, let's have a good look at the lady doctor!"

Then she noticed that others, besides the boys, were staring. As she went through the streets, a knot of well-dressed men or women might gather to look at her, as if she were some strange animal, or a visitor from another planet. Women drew aside their skirts as she passed. A doctor's wife at the boardinghouse table refused to speak to her. It was a long time before she discovered the truth—that people actually believed she was either a bad woman or that, being insane, she would soon show signs of violence. Feeling the un-friendliness, she seldom went out except to the college. It was no sacrifice. Study took up all her time and attention.

Sometimes she became so fascinated with anat-omy that she stayed alone after the others had gone, at least once until nearly midnight. Then she delighted in the walk home, high above the lake, with no staring people, no fluttering curtains at windows, only brisk winter air, clouds, and an expanse of frozen magic glittering in the moonlight.

But anatomy was not all a delight. When Dr. Webster came to his lectures on the reproductive organs, he suggested that she might prefer to be absent. Of course this was an age when such subjects were considered taboo in female society. The doctor had a reputation for treating them with ribaldry in his classes, and he feared her presence would restrict his language.

Elizabeth was both discouraged and dismayed. She had tried hard to make the other students regard her as only one among 150. She had confined herself to a rigid, almost starvation diet, believing that this might keep her from blushing. Now she wrote Dr. Webster that subjects asso-ciated with birth were sacred and should be treated only with reverence. The students were being prepared to officiate at childbirth, a holy ministry in which they would be sharing with women the most intimate mysteries of creation. But if the presence of a woman was embarrassing to him and the class, she would take her seat on a back tier of benches, or, if it was really the desire of the class, she would not attend.

Dr. Webster read her note to the class. She waited for the result in the anteroom, trembling between hope and fear.

Inside the lecture hall the dumpy little doctor suddenly looked six feet tall.

"Gentlemen," he said, "I am humbled. I believe that the noble stand Miss Blackwell has taken entitles her to every privilege that the faculty and class can give her."

Amid a complete silence he opened the door and with courtly dignity ushered Elizabeth to her usual seat. The room shook with applause, and the lecture proceeded without the doctor's customary lewdness and jocularity.

Long afterward Stephen Smith, who became a distinguished physician in New York, wrote that the experience had made him believe in coeducation, even in medical colleges.

But there was plenty of levity in all the news reports about Elizabeth.

"A very notable event of the year 1848," reported the *Boston Medical Journal*, "was the appearance at medical lectures of a young woman student named Blackwell. She is a pretty little specimen of the feminine gender, 26 years of age."

"She should confine her practice," commented the Baltimore *Sun*, "to diseases of the heart."

10

FIRST GRADUATE
WOMAN DOCTOR

A hundred years later a student would have to train for at least three years to receive a degree in medicine, but in 1848 the course consisted of only two sixteen-week terms. Elizabeth's first term ended the last week in January. Nine whole months before she could start another! What to do now? She must fill the time with more training if possible.

She went back to the Elders' house in Philadelphia. What she needed now was medical experience. But how could she get it? The door of every hospital and clinic was closed to her. The answer came suddenly, exciting but terrifying. Blockley! It was a huge almshouse in Philadelphia, with enormous hospital wards—a haven for the poor and outcasts. Her friends were horrified at the idea, but she applied to the board. And, by what seemed a miracle, she was accepted.

She was given a little room on the third floor of the women's hospital in a section containing some of the most diseased patients, who were not only sick, but often unruly. They, as well as the doctors, did not know what to make of her. Sometimes she would hear stealthy footsteps outside her door. She placed her study table in a direct line with the keyhole, so she could satisfy their curiosity. She wanted them to learn to know and trust her.

"You would laugh," she wrote Marian, "to see me wandering eagerly about those great wards, timidly inquiring into symptoms, and looking for useful knowledge. At first it was very trying—all eyes, and such queer eyes, were fixed on my every movement. But already people are becoming accustomed to me."

Not all, however. "I may be poor and cast out by the Lord," one old crone whimpered, "but I'll have no woman to take care of me in my sickness."

The six young doctors resented her. When she walked into a ward, they walked out. They even stopped writing the diagnosis and treatment of the patient's illness on the card at the head of each bed. But the head physician, Dr. Benedict, was both sympathetic and cooperative. Elizabeth thought he was the loveliest man God ever made. Tears came into his eyes as he soothed a dying woman, and his touch was as kind as if each poor patient had been his sister.

She made friends with the matron, the only other "lady" in the establishment. The female nurses, rough and ignorant, could not be called ladies. The matron was a queer combination; she looked like a motherly angel, but her voice would break out in loud scolding. Seated in an armchair in an immense room at the center of the alms-house, she would prop her feet on a velvet footstool, parcel out orders, rave at the paupers, give out clothing, and doom the unruly patients to straitjackets.

Elizabeth was appalled by the suffering of the unhappy patients. Many were unmarried mothers, the helpless victims of men in the households where they had been servants. Yet the women she met in Philadelphia seemed to care little about the injustices these poorer women suffered. They lived frivolous and useless lives.

"Like sweet flowers and bright butterflies," she wrote her sister Emily.

But even as she wrote, the first seeds of the movement for women's rights were being planted. In Seneca Falls, New York, only a few miles from Geneva, three hundred women came to hear Elizabeth Cady Stanton and Lucretia Mott talk of the injustices women endured, how they could not keep their own earnings, manage their own property, share in being guardians to their own children.

News of this convention was sweeping the country, producing horrified reactions from preachers, editors, and other males. What, weaken woman's dependence on man, and so take away one of her liveliest charms?

"The inequality of the sexes," one man protested, "was ordained in Paradise, when God said to woman, 'He shall rule over thee.' Let no woman murmur at the lowliness of her lot."

Elizabeth felt there should be no women's rights and men's rights, only human rights. Women should fight for those not as women but as human beings.

Tragedy came to Blockley when a terrible epidemic of ship fever, a form of typhus, flooded into America with a fresh tide of Irish immigrants. All hands were pressed into service, and even the hostile young doctors welcomed her assistance. She had no fear of catching the disease. Her trust in fresh air and cleanliness was complete. She roamed the wards, trying to find the most effective treatments. Wonderful! She decided to use this subject as her thesis for graduation, and began writing it immediately. What she wrote was to become her lifelong approach to the treatment of disease.

"It is better to prevent disease than to cure it," she believed. "Nature, with its God-given remedies of fresh air, cleanliness, exercise, is the world's best doctor."

Geneva, when she returned in the fall, seemed to have stood still while she had grown older. She plunged into study, spending hours at the tall mahogany medicine cabinet, not even dreaming that a hundred years later it would bear a plaque boasting that it had once been used by Elizabeth Blackwell!

Both time and money must not be wasted, for there was so little of each. She felt as if she were committing a sin if she took up any book or activity unrelated to medicine. And so meager were her resources that she denied herself everything possible. Once she even refused to buy a little bottle of cologne which she wanted badly. She loved perfume. It would have cost perhaps six cents. The memory of that little bottle would haunt her for years.

The students were as courteous and friendly as before. Sometimes, as she sat by the doctor during a demonstration and the students crowded around, she was conscious of their care to keep a respectful distance, drawing back instantly if by accident one of them touched her shoulder.

The townspeople, too, had become indifferent rather than hostile. Though none of the women called on her, they no longer drew aside their skirts or gathered into knots to stare as she passed.

Even the little boys had tired of their old jeers, though sometimes one would think up a new one.

"Doctor, doctor in petticoats, do you cure corns or do you cure colds?"

Graduation day approached. Elizabeth was in agony. Should she have a new dress? Spend five dollars on silk finery? But she would have to mount a platform, where the president would sit in his gown. And some of the family might be coming. She could not disgrace them by appearing in a shabby dress! Finally she had a new gown made, a rich black silk trimmed with silk fringe and lace. A terrible expense, since she was already planning for further medical study!

On January 19 came the final examinations. Suppose she did not pass! As she entered the faculty room to submit to the crucial testing, she felt as if she were approaching the Last Judgment. Familiar as the professors' faces were, they seemed strangers. But the examinations were not too hard, and when she came from the room, so great was her relief that she felt light as air. The men awaiting their turn broke into applause.

"You needn't tell us. They were easy! It's written all over your face."

"Easy for you, maybe. But how about us?"

"Lend me that pretty little head of yours, will you? I'm going to need it."

She was touched by their generosity.

Harry came for the graduation. He went with her to her examinations, and was allowed to attend the session where the graduating class read their theses. Elizabeth, however, did not read hers, for the Buffalo Medical Journal had requested the honor of publishing hers, and it had already been sent to the editor.

Tuesday, January 23, 1849. Elizabeth wakened to a heady mixture of sun and air in almost spring warmth. For a time she lay still, eyes closed, letting the warmth and brilliance seep into her being. Did a bride feel like this on her wedding day? Or a nun on the morning she was to take the veil? You had sweated and strained and climbed for what seemed an eternity. Then suddenly you were there at the top of the mountain. But how stupid! As if this day were an end instead of a beginning!

It occurred to Elizabeth that Harry was still in town, and they were going to the graduation. She sprang up and closed the window. She dressed carefully, reluctantly lacing her stays tight to fit the wasp-waisted style. She adjusted the heavy corset of cotton and donned the new padded and quilted woolen petticoat. She topped all with the new black gown and cape and drew on her long black gloves. Shortly after she had dressed Harry arrived, and they left.

In front of the college Dr. Webster swooped toward them, his open academic gown flapping like wings. "My dear Miss Blackwell, you really must march with us! It's your procession of triumph, you know."

"I'm sorry, Dr. Webster." Elizabeth spoke firmly. "I couldn't. It wouldn't be ladylike."

He looked surprised. A queer reaction from a woman who had defied centuries of rocklike tradition! "Why— no— I suppose it wouldn't," he said.

The streets were swarming with crowds, but Elizabeth was puzzled because there seemed to be no women. Were they staying away because of her? Well! She set her shoulders and lifted her small head a little higher. Let them! She was used to their disapproval.

Graduation was to be held in the Presbyterian Church. It stood about four hundred yards from the location of a sign erected in 1932 by the state of New York which would say: *Site of Geneva Medical College. Eliz. Blackwell received here the first degree of M.D. ever conferred upon a woman.*

Entering the church on Harry's arm, Elizabeth felt engulfed in a flood of female gowns and bonnets. No wonder she had seen no women on the street! They were all here, crowding the seats, leaving hardly enough pews for the graduating class! They must have come from miles around. Her entrance was greeted by a flurry of whispers, a rustle of silk dresses, and a swiveling of bonnets.

The old shyness overwhelmed her, and she felt herself blushing. Then suddenly she straightened. Her head lifted. This was one of the reasons why she was here, to show other women that they could be different. She was glad they were curious.

Harry felt the change in her and smiled. It was one of those times when little Bessie seemed ten feet tall. Seated beside Harry, Elizabeth remembered the presence which had filled her room with light that long ago night in Asheville. This was a holy hour.

There was a burst of martial music as the procession entered. A student in her class stopped at her pew and offered her his arm. She joined the march up the aisle and took her seat with the others. Feeling every eye upon her, she removed her bonnet, and got ready for the big moment.

President Hale, in his velvet cap, seated himself as the graduates came to the platform, four at a time, to receive their diplomas. Elizabeth was last.

"Domina Blackwell." This time the president

removed his cap and stood up. He presented the diploma amid utter silence.

Elizabeth bowed and started to leave the platform, then on a sudden impulse she turned back.

"Sir," she said in a low clear voice, "I thank you. By the help of God, it shall be the effort of my life to shed honor upon your diploma."

Elizabeth put on her bonnet, and tied the strings. Harry held her cape, smiling. "Permit me, *Doctor* Blackwell."

One hand tucked through his arm, the other clutched the precious diploma. She swept down the aisle and out of the church. Almost all the ladies had stopped outside. Now they opened their ranks to let her pass through. Many of the faces she recognized. She had seen them turning away in church, or on the streets coldly staring. She did not return their smiles and nods, merely passed through as if they had not existed. Not that she intended to be catty or spiteful. It was just that their approval no longer mattered.

The news of her graduation swept the country. It aroused almost as much publicity as the 1849 Gold Rush. Newspapers expressed wonder, disbelief, amusement, ridicule, dismay, outrage, approval. There was not much of the latter.

"It is to be regretted," wrote the *Boston Medical and Surgical Journal*, "that Miss Blackwell has been induced to depart from the appropriate sphere of her sex and led to aspire to honors and duties which, by the order of nature and the common consent of the world, devolve upon men."

England also reported the event. The magazine *Punch* published a rollicking poem, which began:

Young ladies all, of every clime,
Especially of Britain;

I Will Be a Doctor!

Who wholly occupy your time
In novels or in knitting,
Whose highest skill is but to play,
Sing, dance or French to clack well,
Reflect on the example, pray,
Of excellent Miss Blackwell!

11

ROMANCE IN PARIS

What to do now? She had her diploma —her medical degree. She had reached her first goal to become a full-fledged doctor. But she was not ready to practice medicine. She had never performed an operation or personally delivered a baby. Her classmates would be able to find positions as interns in hospitals and get further instruction under a qualified physician. But not a woman. No reputable hospital would admit her.

Paris! That was the solution. All her medical friends advised it as the place for offering unlimited training. And by a happy coincidence a cousin, Kenyon Blackwell, who was visiting from England and had met her in Philadelphia, was urging her to go back to Europe with him. He even offered to advance funds for her expenses. Anna was now in Europe writing for American newspapers, and that was a further inducement. She began brushing up her French in preparation for possible study in Paris.

After some time in Philadelphia, listening to lectures and taking a course in dissection she went home in March, after nearly five years' absence. It was wonderful to see Mamma again, though it was hard persuading her that life could contain any more worthwhile goal than marriage. She marveled over George and Ellen, grown beyond recognition. She rejoiced with Sam over his purchase of a new hardware business, and delighted once more in Marian's delicate beauty, but agonized over her ill health.

But it was Emily now, not Marian, with whom she felt the strongest kindship, for Emily now had a consuming desire to become a doctor. She fired questions and demanded details. In their long walks together Elizabeth gave them to her, omitting none of the difficulties.

Yet in spite of their joys the ten days at home seemed too long. She was like a racehorse waiting for the starting gun to sound.

"You can't guess how much I long to be at work," she confided to Sam.

She left by boat on Saturday, April 2, 1849. The whole family came to see her off for Pittsburgh. Elizabeth watched them through a blur of tears until the curve of the river hid them. But already her sights were set far beyond Pittsburgh, even beyond Philadelphia, where she spent several days with the Elders. On April 13 her naturalization paper was granted, and she became an American citizen. Five days later she sailed with Cousin Kenyon for England.

The year of 1849 was one of great change in Europe. The word "freedom" was on every tongue. France had just declared iself a republic. Germany and Italy had begun a struggle for freedom. In England there had been serious riots by people demanding more rights.

But at the country estate of Uncle Blackwell, whom she remembered from childhood, nothing seemed changed. Even Uncle himself, with his white hair and rosy face, was just as she remembered him seventeen years ago. Anna was there, as sparkling and generous, but as sharp-edged, as ever.

Elizabeth went alone to London, and was surprised and delighted by her cordial reception from the medical world.

"You should spend a year in London," one doctor told her. "Here almost every new idea is represented."

Elizabeth was tempted, but she wanted to become a surgeon, and Paris seemed the place to study. She sailed for France on May 20 with plans to come back to England later.

Paris! It was indeed the center of art, fashion, music, and medicine! But also of political turmoil and disease. When she arrived cholera was raging. Already more than fifteen thousand had died of it.

She soon found a small apartment with a friendly landlady, and Anna joined her there. A Boston doctor had given Elizabeth a letter of introduction to the great Pierre Charles Alexandre Louis, one of the great medical teachers of the world. She sent him the letter and waited in an agony of suspense. Would he see her? To her amazement the very next day the great Louis, a tall, imposing gentleman, called on her. But after telling him her desire to study medicine and surgery, her hopes sank.

"Miss Blackwell," he said, "I would advise you to enter La Maternité. There you can obtain invaluable knowledge in obstetrics."

Elizabeth felt as if he had dashed cold water in her face. He did not think of her as a doctor but as a midwife, one of those women who through the ages had been given the task of officiating at the birth of children! Her hopes sank like lead.

He was like all the rest, believing that women had no business trying to be real doctors.

But after he had gone she began to think. It was experience she needed, and La Maternité was the biggest lying-in hospital (serving expectant mothers) in the world. She would have to postpone her studies in surgery, but the time would not be wasted. A doctor should certainly know all about delivering babies! However, she would consider La Maternité only as a last resort.

She applied to every one of the principal hospitals for an internship, and was refused. La Maternité seemed the only solution. But when she investigated it, she was appalled. It would be almost like going to prison! Visitors were allowed only once a week. She would have poor food and lodging, and lose three or four nights of sleep each week. But—what benefits! Experience with many hundreds of cases, lectures from the most noted professors of obstetrics. Worth the sacrifice? A thousand times yes!

She had no idea of the commotion her presence in Paris had caused.

"The medical community is all agog at the arrival of the celebrated American doctor, Miss Elizabeth Blackwell," one paper reported. "She has quite bewildered the learned faculty by her diploma authorizing her to dose, bleed, and amputate. Some think she must be a rabid socialist. She is young and rather good looking."

La Maternité accepted her, not as a doctor, as a pupil. She was on a par with sixty to eighty young French women students. Most of them were poor girls in their teens or early twenties from the country. Some were almost illiterate. Elizabeth was not even allowed a room by herself or permission to go out occasionally.

Anna rode with her to the hospital. A high stone wall showed the tops of old buildings jutting above it. They entered through a very small door, and an old woman led them through many passages to the parlor of Madame Charrier, the midwife-in-chief. Madame was tiny, deformed, and old, but with cheeks as smooth and bright as painted china. Elizabeth was relieved to see kindness in her blue eyes.

Anna left tearfully and Madame took Elizabeth to Madame Blockel, superintendent of the dormitories. She was a little woman with squinting black eyes. She wore a black gown and cap and was muffled in an old shawl. She took Elizabeth to the student infirmary.

"You will sleep here until we can make other arrangements."

Elizabeth was not pleased. She looked suspiciously at the long rows of beds with their white curtains drawn. What sort of diseases might they hide? Her trunk was brought up, her bed shown to her, and she was left alone. Hastily she pulled aside each curtain, and to her relief found every bed empty but one. On it lay a student who had a headache. They talked together.

"Are you from my province?" asked the girl eagerly.

Elizabeth was flattered. Her French must be good if she sounded like a native. Finding that she was an American who had lived in New York, the only place in America she had heard of, the girl was much excited.

"Is that an island near Havana?" she inquired. Elizabeth discovered later that the pupils were disappointed because she was not black, as they thought all persons from America were Negroes!

She went to work that night in the delivery

room. Putting on a big apron of coarse toweling, she felt more than ever like a novice taking a nun's veil. The delivery room was large and dim, with beds all around, and a fire on the hearth. In the center there was a large wooden table on which the newborn babies would be placed tightly swathed and labeled.

During the night eight new babies appeared. It was an amazing sight—eight little red faces, each peeping from under a coarse, peaked cap marked with name and sex. Each wore a black serge jacket with a white handerchief pinned across it, and a small blanket tightly folded around the rest of the body. They looked like tiny mummies.

Elizabeth went off duty at ten the next morning, tired but triumphant. In a single night she had gained more practical knowledge of childbirth than in all her years of study!

The next night she moved into a sixteen-bed dormitory. She shoved her narrow iron bed forward and fitted her one chair behind, so that it was next to a window. She hung up her dressing gown and put a few books on the floor behind her. Here she enjoyed a "study," with plenty of fresh air and just enough room to write.

At five each morning she was jolted awake by a loud bell. She sprang out of bed, and after washing (an act which astonished her fellow students), she put on her big white apron with its huge pocket. She hastened to wash her patients, and see that their beds were arranged. Then with the other students she went with Madame Charrier on her rounds. Hurrying back to the dormitory, she made her bed, snatched a crust of bread, and rushed to the classroom for Madame's seven o'clock lesson.

Rounds . . . lectures. She would not have missed

a moment of them. Dr. Dubois was a gentle bald little man who was a wonderful teacher.

"You should stay a year and gain the gold medal," he told her one day. "You would be the best midwife in America!"

"But I already have a medical degree," she said, "from a reputable college." She could tell by his smile that he considered the word "reputable" unlikely.

One day Madame Charrier summoned Elizabeth. In her hand was an account of a surgical case that Elizabeth had observed and made notes on.

"You wrote this report, Mademoiselle?"

"Yes, Madame."

"It is good! A doctor could not have done better."

"But I am—" Elizabeth stopped and smiled ruefully. Madame knew she had a medical degree, yet it was incredible to her that a woman could function as a doctor.

Elizabeth had plunged into this new experience with all her energy and enthusiasm. She had expected, wanted every part of herself to be involved—mind, eyes, hands, feet, but not her heart.

Her first meeting with a handsome young intern, Hippolyte Blot, had been wholly impersonal, though in the delivery room she had noticed his careful hands, his sober, almost too perfect features. Then there were the Tuesday vaccinations. A space would be cleared in the nurses' hall, and Blot would sit there with his vaccines and knives.

One Tuesday it was Elizabeth's task to hold each screaming little patient as Monsieur Blot used his knife. Sometimes she would ask him a question, but each time she did so he blushed, passed his hand through his hair, and avoided her gaze in such an un-Frenchmanlike manner that she stopped disturbing him. Was he embarrassed? Disapproving? Or— could he possibly be in awe of her? It did not occur to her that he might be attracted to her as a woman.

Not long afterward he loaned her a medical journal. Some days later he approached her, blushing, but with determination. "I wonder, Mademoiselle, if you would consider giving me lessons in English."

For some reason Elizabeth felt herself blushing. "Of course. I would be most happy."

So began a pleasant relationship. Sometimes Elizabeth would remain after his class, and they would talk together in both languages. They discussed medical subjects. These hours were the happiest of her days. Yet they also aroused envy and frustration. Hippolyte was writing his thesis.

"If I should get a gold medal," he confided, "I could enter any hospital here in Paris I choose as an intern."

Elizabeth felt secretly resentful. What chance did a woman have? In sudden defiance she told him of her own determination to become a surgeon, and, though he was gallantly polite, she could see the look of skepticism in his eyes. He might as well have said, "What! A woman surgeon?"

Just when Elizabeth made her troublesome discovery she was not sure. Perhaps it was the moment when she sensed that she was too conscious of the dark head bent close to hers over the miroscope. As soon as possible she fled to her room, cheeks burning. So— she was in love again. Again? No. Never had she felt such emotion as this before. It was the ideal relationship of a man and woman, made up of trust, admiration, and mutual interest. She knew that at that moment she would gladly sacrifice everything she had paid such a price for, if she could become the cherished, obedient, yes, even subservient wife of Hippolyte Blot.

The moment passed, and cool reason came. Even if he shared her emotion, marriage was out of the question. A Frenchman, a promising young doctor, breaking all the rules of family, tradition, to marry a Protestant foreigner frowned on by his profession? Impossible. It might ruin his career. And what about herself?

"But Hippolyte would never expect me to give up my career," she told herself. "Surely we could work together."

"Not as doctors," reason argued back. "Doctor and midwife perhaps. Is that what you've worked for all these years, sacrificed for?"

Questions, with no answers. She lay down and must have slept, for she roused to feel her shoulders being shaken.

"Mademoiselle! Come. An operation!"

She staggered to her feet, pulled on her clothes, and followed the nurse's oil lamp through the maze of corridors to the operating theater. It must be a big operation for other students had been aroused.

It was big— and painful. The patient was already stretched on the stained cot, which served as a table. Couldn't they even give the poor thing a clean sheet to lie on, Elizabeth wondered. The surgeon put on his dirty operating coat and took his instruments from an old cloth bag. He wiped each one on his coat, and laid them on a table. He reached for his scalpel, dropped it on the floor, scolded the nervous nurse who picked it up, and without cleaning it plunged it into the body of the patient. Neither the gag in her mouth nor the pounding rain on the glass skylight smothered her cries of pain.

Elizabeth did not faint like some of the others, but it was the most painful hour she had ever spent. Surgery need not be like that, she decided. The poor woman could have been given privacy and shown a bit of tenderness. When she became a surgeon, she vowed, she would at least wear a clean coat and wash her instruments.

It was hard after that attending Hippolyte Blot's lectures and staying afterward to teach him English. It would have been harder if his manner had ever indicated more than friendliness. Only once did their conversation turn toward romance.

"Sometimes one's family is a nuisance! Mine is getting impatient. They want to arrange for me a marriage!"

"Well, after all, you are—" She wondered if he could hear the beating of her heart. "You are older than most Frenchmen when they marry."

"I am twenty-six," he replied.

She felt a swift relief. He was only two years younger than herself. As if that mattered, she told herself. He was a good friend, nothing more. Her divine calling was to find some way to train in surgery, and nothing on earth was going to stop her.

12
TRAGEDY

But something did stop her. It was still dark at five o'clock on a November morning. Elizabeth struggled out of bed and went to make the rounds of her patients. One of them was a baby with a bad case of ophthalmia, a highly contagious eye ailment.

"Poor mite," she murmured as she bent over the tiny swaddled shape with the eye syringe. She had to lean far over the crib in the dim light of the smoky lamp, and somehow a little of the fluid that she had injected spurted into her own left eye. She washed it out carefully, knowing how even a small drop from the infected eye might be dangerous. Then in the bustle of her duties she forgot about it.

The next morning her eye was painfully inflamed. Panic stricken, she had only one thought—Hippolyte Blot. She went straight to the infirmary, where he was working. He examined her eyes gently and confirmed her fears. Yes, it was the dreaded disease, which was terribly infectious and sometimes resulted in blindness.

"The next few days," he said, "may well determine whether you completely recover."

She was put to bed in the infirmary, and

Hippolyte got permission to devote all of his time to her. Though some of the treatments were painful, she tried to keep calm. Pain was unimportant beside the terrible possibility of losing the sight of her eye. She came to know Hippolyte's quiet step, and her heart hammered at his approach.

One night she was asleep when he came. Drifting slowly awake, she thought she must still be dreaming, for often in her dreams she had heard him speaking those very words.

"Cherie! Ma pauvre cherie! (Dear! My poor dear!)"

She lay very still. He must not know she had heard. Then she stirred. "Oh, I didn't hear you come! I must have been asleep."

When he had gone she lay trembling. He had spoken not in pity but in tenderness. So—Hippolyte loved her! Whatever the future might do to her, she would always have the memory of this hour of pain-mingled happiness.

But it was only an hour. For nothing had really changed. Marriage to Hippolyte was still impossible. And even if it hadn't been, there was her career as a doctor that must come first in her life.

She was awake when he came again. After he had treated her eye she reached for his hand.

"How can I ever repay you for all you're doing for me?" she said. "I must confess I can't help thinking of you as more than a friend." Feeling his hand tense, she hurried on. "You seem to me more like a brother. I told you I have four brothers. Now I feel I have five."

There was a long silence. When he finally spoke his voice was unsteady. "Thank you, Mademoiselle."

"Mon frere. My brother." She applied a little

pressure before releasing his hand. "And I hope you will think of me as your sister."

"Mademoiselle—" He sounded as if he wanted to say more.

"Please— sister!"

There was another silence.

"Very well. I am honored. Good night, *ma soeur*, my sister."

He was gone. Now she could hardly tell where the pain in her eye left off and that in her heart began.

Three days passed. Three weeks. And the eye still pained. There was no morning, no night. Everything was darkness. Then came more weeks of waiting. It might be six weeks before she knew if she had lost the sight of her eye. Every two hours Hippolyte Blot would come and treat her. Everything possible was done. Though everyone tried to talk to give her hope, she could hear the doubt in their voices.

After three more weeks her right eye began gradually to open, though she could still see very little with it. However, she could get up and move around enough to take care of some of her needs.

Bandaged and veiled, she left La Maternité the last of November. There were sorrowful good-byes. Madame Charrier's kind eyes were bright with tears, and Hippolyte Blot kissed her hand.

Anna had an apartment in Paris, so Elizabeth had a place to go. In the apartment she looked in a mirror for the first time since the accident. Her pale face was thin, and the infected eye shocked her into numbed horror. When Hippolyte came the next day to give her a treatment, he saw her calmness suddenly shattered.

"Tell me, is there any hope?"

His silence was louder than words. "My dear

Mademoiselle," he said finally with great gentleness, "whatever life brings to us, there is always hope."

"Thank you," she said quietly.

That night she and Anna wept together, and for two days Elizabeth lived in despair. Then slowly hope returned. Hippolyte must be wrong. It was impossible that a little accident like this could affect her whole life purpose! When he came the next Sunday, he found her again calm and confident.

But weeks lengthened into months, and there was little improvement. Though her right eye grew steadily stronger, using it aggravated the weakness of the left. Yet the months were not wasted. She hired a student to drill her in anatomy and attended lectures at a medical college. Once more everything seemed possible. She *would* become a surgeon.

But not without two eyes. One day in late May she faced the truth. It was the day a letter came from England saying she was admitted as a student in surgery at St. Bartholomew's Hospital, one of the best in London. Her first triumph burst like a bubble. She went to a mirror, looked into it, then covered her right eye and turned toward the window. Its light was very faint. She knew she had lost the sight in that eye. She could never be a surgeon. She felt as if a door had been slammed in her face.

But worse was yet to come. One morning she woke in violent pain. A famous eye specialist confirmed her fears. The eye must be removed.

The surgery was performed on August 15. After that her right eye grew still stronger, and an artificial eye made her look almost as if nothing had happened. At least she could still be a doctor! Joyously she left for England in October.

At St. Bartholomew's she was allowed to visit all the wards and to follow the doctors on their rounds. They were for the most part friendly, and she was only excluded from the department that treated "women's diseases!"

She made many congenial friends in England. One of them came to visit her at her boarding-house. Though Elizabeth had met her before, this was the first chance they had had to get really acquainted. Her name alone was enough to arouse interest—*Florence*. A queer name, Elizabeth thought, given her because of the city in Italy where she had been born, but it suited her. The oval face in its halo of rich brown hair and silk bonnet seemed to suggest marble statues and Italian paintings. Elizabeth did not know at this time that because of this young woman hundreds of children would soon be bearing the name. She was Florence Nightingale.

"I had to come," the visitor said. "There are so many things I have to ask you, about yourself, your study, your home, and your family. Especially your family. I hope you won't think I'm meddlesome, but I have to know. What did they think of your studying medicine?"

Elizabeth did not think her meddlesome. This girl, she discovered, was determined to become a nurse, an unheard-of occupation for an English-woman of good family. Nurses were usually women of low repute. They had no other home than the filthy, noisy wards where they slept, lived and even cooked their meals. No wonder the rich and aristocratic Nightingale family had shuddered at their daughter's thinking of such a career!

Elizabeth spoke of her family and how they had loyally supported her venture.

"Suppose," said Florence when she had finished, "they had not approved. Suppose they had fought you at every turn. What then?"

Elizabeth hesitated. What should she say? She had been told about Florence's family, their horror at her dream of going to Kaiserswerth, a religious training school for nurses in Germany. Her answer, she knew, was terribly important. It might change the course of a life. But she knew she must be honest.

"It would have made no difference," she said firmly. "I would have done it just the same."

Suddenly her visitor's face was transformed. She burst into the sweetest smile imaginable.

"Thank you," said Florence joyously.

When Elizabeth had finished her study in London, Florence was one of those who begged her to stay in England.

"Please! Don't go back to America. Stay here and let me work with you. When I come back from Germany—Oh, yes, I'm really going!—I'm going to have a hospital. I'm going to teach other women, good women, to be nurses. We can work together. That will make me so happy."

Elizabeth was tempted. She loved England, her native land. But there were strong reasons why she should not stay. She had no money and a horror of running into debt. Here there was no immediate family to help her. Besides, she believed firmly that it was in America, not Europe, that woman would first be recognized as man's equal. In America women were already organizing and making themselves heard. Marian wrote of a big women's rights convention that she and Ellen had attended in Massachusetts. The Elders reported that a medical school *for women* had actually been started in Philadelphia. Yes, it was back in America that she wanted to start her work as a doctor.

13

BEGINNINGS

"**B**ut— you advertised rooms for the use of a doctor!" Drawing herself up to her full five feet plus, Elizabeth fixed her cool gaze on the landlady.

The woman looked outraged. "A *doctor*. Not a woman."

"But I *am* a doctor. Here, I will show you my diploma."

But before Elizabeth could open her bag to take it out, the door slammed. She sighed and turned away. The same thing had happened a dozen times in the past month.

"Female doctor!" one woman said. "You think I run *that* kind of a house?"

Elizabeth returned wearily to her lodgings on Bleecker Street.

Had she been wrong to come to New York? In London at least she could have found a place to work. People there would have been indifferent, but not hostile. As soon as she had arrived in New York she had made application to become one of the doctors in a large city dispensary. She had submitted her credentials from Geneva, Paris, London, and letters from some of the distinguished English doctors.

"We have all the help we need," she was told curtly.

But at last she was able to find rooms at Number 44 University Place. However, she had to rent a whole floor of the house at a price far higher than she could afford. Fortunately her sisters had submitted a story Elizabeth had written called "Aunt Esther" in a magazine contest, and it had won a prize of a hundred dollars. It was like a gift from heaven. In spite of the landlady's horrified objections she hung out her modest shingle: ELIZABETH BLACKWELL, M.D. At least now she had a place to receive patients.

But how could she persuade them to come? After waiting for someone to read her sign and come, she got an idea. Horace Greeley, the editor of the New York *Tribune,* a paper which Anna wrote for, was a well-known liberal. She went to see him, introducing herself as Anna's sister.

"I know you are a liberal," she told him bluntly. "But are you liberal enough to publish an advertisement for a woman doctor?"

Mr. Greeley was. The next day he printed an announcement of her office's opening and listed her credentials. A few weeks later he published another item:

"We lately announced the establishment of Miss Blackwell in our city as a practitioner at Number 44 University Place. We are happy to learn that she is extremely successful."

Pure wishful thinking! That fall and winter were a nightmare of discouragement. Without the small sums of money her brothers were able to send her she could not have managed. She counted the lumps of coal and nearly starved herself, while both courage and money dwindled. Everything seemed against her. She asked to visit hospitals, but was refused. No doctor would recognize her as a member of the profession. Should she have gone to Philadelphia instead of New York? At least Dr. Warrington was there. Perhaps she should give up and go now. No. She had chosen New York, and she would not be defeated!

In the evenings, discouraged and lonely, she walked, and everywhere she saw problems that concerned her. If she walked east, toward the East River, there were the slum sections filled with immigrants from Ireland and Germany. She longed to do something about their poverty and their terrible lack of sanitation. Elizabeth was generations ahead of her time in believing that uncleanliness was a cause of disease.

Walking south toward the Bowery, she saw thousands of filthy, half-naked children, picking rags and bones from the street. She was almost mobbed by screaming candy and match peddlers and newsboys. Most of them, she found out, had been orphaned by cholera, tuberculosis, or starvation.

"If only I could help them in some way!" she thought.

Walking uptown, she was also disturbed. Fashionable ladies floated along Fifth Avenue in billowing hoops, waists pinched in by tight corsets, and pale faces covered by veils. The young girls were as tightly laced as their mothers.

"Don't their mothers know anything about keeping healthy?" she asked herself.

If not, then she must tell them. Hour after hour she wrote, tore up, rewrote, weighing each word carefully, for people did not talk about the things she was writing. At last she was satisfied. On March 1, 1852, the *New York Times* announced that

Dr. Elizabeth Blackwell would give a course of six lectures in a church basement on "The Laws of Life with Special Reference to the Physical Education of Girls." Tickets would be two dollars each.

She went to the first meeting terrified. She had never made a speech in her life. Would anyone come? If they came, would they be willing to listen? Though she looked perfectly calm, under the black silk skirts her legs were shaking.

Some women came, many of them belonging to the Society of Friends, sometimes called Quakers. To her surprise, once she started talking she became less nervous. She told them that life should be a unity of body and spirit. God wanted people to be healthy as well as holy.

"See that your girls exercise when children," she told them. "When they get older, free them from those strangling corsets and swathing veils. Let them enjoy fresh air and sunshine. Train them in skills that will give them worthwhile goals in life. We need courses in all schools and colleges in science and sanitation."

Then—shocking idea!—she gave them instruction in the processes of sex, birth, and of the structure and functions of their bodies! A daring act in this era when it was not considered proper to even mention the word "body"! Some of the women got up and left. Others stayed to the end, but did not come back. But many returned for more.

And they got it. She told them what she had seen in the back streets of New York: the overcrowded tenements, the dirty unwholesome food, the terrible diseases, and the children who had no homes except wooden boxes in back alleys. She always emphasized respect for the human body, which was another kind of respect for the human spirit.

"Those lectures must be published in a book," insisted Mrs. Collins, the wife of a prominent Quaker publisher. And they were. Many were shocked, but others gave it hearty praise. One of the letters Elizabeth treasured was from Dr. Lee, her teacher in Geneva.

"I would not flatter you," he wrote, "but I hope I may say that in my judgment you have done yourself and Alma Mater a very great honor, and rendered a most important service to your sex and to society at large."

Her pleasure in this letter was a bit spoiled because he had addressed it to "Miss" not "Dr." Blackwell!

More people were horrified than approving. In those years of the 1850s people had no idea that cleanliness was necessary for good health. They regarded the body as evil, and sex as an unmentionable vice. The fact that a woman knew enough and was bold enough to write about such things made them even more disapproving of a woman doctor.

"It has taken fifty years," one of America's first child specialists was to say a half century later, "for even the foremost of the medical profession to catch up with Dr. Blackwell's ideas."

Patients began to come. Some of them were the women who had heard her lectures. But this only made people more hostile. Her landlady refused to give or receive messages.

"That shingle," she announced, "is a blot on my house. You must take it down. No respectable woman would want to live in a house with a woman doctor."

Elizabeth began receiving insulting letters. Obscene words were flung after her as she walked along the street. It was the persecution of Geneva all over again. But why? Why should people think a woman doctor was such an evil person, a woman of loose morals? Yet she was glad it was she and not someone less strong and hardened who had to do this work of pioneering, someone like her little sister Emily.

Emily was also determined to become a doctor. She had worked, scrimped, and saved for years for her medical education. Unfortunately, she had been turned down by a dozen medical schools, including Geneva, for Dr. Lee was no longer there. Now she came to visit Elizabeth. Emily was so much younger that Elizabeth did not feel she really knew her well. Anxiously, with some doubting, she regarded her sister's face appraisingly. It was rounder than her own, prettier, calmer, revealing little of emotion.

"How strong is she?" Elizabeth wondered. "Does she have the strength to batter this terrible iron wall?"

But Emily also had her worries. She remembered Elizabeth's strong will, her stubborness, and her urge to get her own way. *Could we work together later?* she wondered.

But now they seemed to be in perfect accord. They spent a week together, one of the happiest Elizabeth had known. Then Emily left to apply at Dartmouth in New Hampshire. A week later she was back again. She had been refused. Her calmness was shattered. She was in despair. Elizabeth was not surprised.

But then for Emily there came a seeming miracle. That fall Rush Medical college admitted her, and Emily left for Chicago.

Elizabeth had other family worries. Her brother Harry was now a fairly successful businessman, whose travels sometimes brought him to New York. In many ways he was still the roguish boy she had always known, his blue eyes innocent and sparkling. He had been in and out of love a half dozen times, and always unfortunate in his choices. His latest attachment, Elizabeth felt, was the most unfortunate of all. He was in love with Lucy Stone, a feminist and abolitionist. Not that Elizabeth did not agree with movements for women's rights and freedom of the slaves, but she doubted if any woman who ran all over the country, wearing bloomers and making speeches, could be a good wife and mother.

Lucy Stone had captured Harry, as she did her audiences, by her beauty, charm, and eloquence; but she was determined not to marry. Harry ruefully told Elizabeth about his first meeting with Lucy, when he had gone to her home in West Brookfield, Massachusetts, and climbed the hill to her family's farmhouse.

He found Lucy in a short dress, standing on a table whitewashing the ceiling of her parents' living room. She greeted him cordially, having heard of his antislavery interest, and they walked together to the top of the hill above the house. Harry urged her to come west and lecture, offering to make all the arrangments. He also told her that he wanted to make her his wife.

Lucy was both kind and frank. "Thank you for the honor, Mr. Blackwell. But I have consecrated myself to work for women's rights and have resolved never to marry."

Harry was not discouraged. "But I also believe firmly in women's equality with men. We might work better together than you could alone."

She did not agree, but she did allow him to arrange lectures for her and promised to exchange letters with him. So began Harry's long and difficult courtship of Lucy Stone.

Her brother Samuel was causing her no such worries. Sober, studious, and deeply religious, he was well established in a hardware business in Cincinnati and showed no signs of romantic involvement.

In September 1853 New York was to hold a great exhibition, and Elizabeth had a chance to see Lucy Stone at a women's rights convention. With Lucy was a friend, Antoinette Brown, the first woman to be ordained into the Christian ministry. Her ordination had been denounced by every newspaper.

"Any woman who would allow herself to be ordained," declared the New York *Independent,* "is an infidel!"

Antoinette had brought a letter from her Congregational church to one of the conventions, which gave her a right to speak. But when she rose to do so the meeting broke into an uproar. For two hours she stood on the platform waiting in vain for order.

Elizabeth's old friend Harriet Beecher Stowe wrote about the incident, "If it is right for Jenny Lind to *sing* to two thousand people, 'I Know that My Redeemer Liveth', is it wrong for Antoinette Brown to *say* the same thing?"

Elizabeth heartily agreed. She admired Antoinette and felt toward her none of the strange antagonism she felt toward Lucy Stone. Why? Because of her striking beauty, poise and calm, in contrast with Lucy's dominating liveliness? Or was it because she did not threaten the happiness of the Blackwell family?

Elizabeth, of course, could not know that three years later Antoinette Brown would become Mrs. Samuel Blackwell!

14

START ONE YOURSELF!

In her own career Elizabeth was feeling more and more frustrated. She had a few patients, but they were not the sort who really needed her. What was she doing about the suffering of women in the teeming society about her? Nothing. Yet she knew they were in desperate need of the skills she had to give. She must do something.

That same year of 1853 she went again to the directors of the city dispensary, asking for a place on its staff. They were even more curt in their refusal.

"If you want to work in a dispensary, start one yourself."

"Thank you," she replied calmly, "I will do just that."

With the help of some of her Quaker friends she rented a cheap room on Seventh street near Tompkins Square. Elizabeth announced that she would receive patients there on three afternoons each week and treat them—free. A modest sign bore the words, Dr. Blackwell.

It was one of the worst slum districts in the city. There was no medical service of any kind. Most of the people were foreigners. Families of ten or twelve existed in one or two rooms. Garbage was flung into the narrow alleys. Herds of pigs roamed the streets. The smell was almost more than Elizabeth could bear.

"But it's only a few hours a week for me," she told herself. "These women, my sisters, who live here have it all the time."

A woman doctor was as suspect here as on Madison Avenue, but finally a patient came, so sick that the word "doctor" made her forget her fears. Elizabeth was able to help her, and the grateful woman told others. Women soon were swarming to the little dispensary. Elizabeth was overwhelmed with work. She was called at all hours and into all sorts of places, often to deliver babies. More than once she found the patient lying in a cellar on a heap of burlap bags. A ragged, whimpering bunch of children usually clustered around her. The death rate of babies was appalling.

She did more than treat sickness and deliver babies. She lectured the mothers.

"Give your babies fresh air and sunlight, give them wholesome food, exercise them, and wash them with soap and water."

Of course she had little success, but it was something. However, there were more problems. Gossip increased. Her visits to patients' homes, often at night through dark streets and alleys, were sometimes unpleasant. A well-dressed man might walk by her side along Broadway, saying in a low voice, "Turn down the next street to the right." When she walked ahead with no sign of hearing him, he would vanish in the dark. Always, she discovered, with common sense and self-reliance any woman could do her work as a doctor without undue risk. But not without loneliness and pain! She had always resented the gossip and the falsehoods.

"I understand now," she thought, "why this life has been shunned by women. It is hard. I should like a little fun now and then."

Elizabeth was lonely, but by no means idle. The little dispensary was taking up more and more of her time. There should be a place open at all times, not just a few days a week. And—her head swam with new ideas—there should be a place for training other workers, women nurses and—dare she dream of it?—women doctors! Hesitantly and fearfully, she went to some of her new friends. Would they be willing to back her in the plan, willing even to become trustees of a new dispensary if she had it incorporated?

She was amazed and humbled by their swift agreement, because she knew it would make them unpopular with most people. Some of them were very important, lawyers, editors, merchants. There were even a few doctors who agreed to be consultants. The new dispensary at 207 East Seventh Street was opened in March of 1854.

Elizabeth had another dream. She wanted a house all her own. If only the family could be with her at least part of the time instead of scattered and far away! George, Sam, and Harry could all find some good work in New York. Ellen could study the art she loved. Marian could keep house for them, and Mamma could fuss and worry and watch over them. Huddled in shawls and blankets to save on precious fuel, Elizabeth dreamed, hoped, and planned.

Well—why not? The rented rooms were all expense and she had almost no income. Her landlady was becoming more and more hostile. She must buy a house! She finally found one on

East Fifteenth Street, and a friend loaned her the funds to buy it. It was too big, but she rented most of it to a family that kept boarders, and kept for herself only a front room for an office and a bedroom-kitchen in the attic. Proudly she hung her shingle on the front of the house. Now no landlady—nobody—could tell her to take it down!

Still life was lonely. It would be a long time before any of the family could join her permanently. But at last Emily graduated from the medical school at Western Reserve Medical College in Cleveland, where she had gone after being ousted from Chicago. She had won incredible honors. The highest number of points usually given a student was ten. Emily was rated eleven!

One doctor who had been opposed to her admission said to one of the faculty, "This is the only student you have passed, whom I could introduce to practice in my family."

When Emily came to New York Elizabeth felt that her cup of happiness was full. They worked together in the infirmary. But it was not to last.

"I need to know more," Emily decided. "I want to go to England and study."

Elizabeth's heart sank, but at the same time her hopes soared.

"Of course you must go. Some of the best teaching doctors in the world are in England and Scotland. And— my dear—" She was all hopes now, not disappointed, "you must do what I was unable to do—become a *surgeon!*"

Emily agreed. But she had seen the disappointmen in Elizabeth's eyes, and knew the loneliness that her leaving would bring back.

"I have an idea," she said one day. "Why don't you take a little orphan girl and train her as a servant? It would keep her off the streets or out of a wretched asylum, and give you some of the help you can't afford to hire. And she would be company for you."

"I'll consider it," Elizabeth replied, "but reluctantly."

Emily left for England and Scotland, and Elizabeth felt as if she had been left alone on a desert island. But the letters that kept coming back brought almost incredible good news. Emily was working as an assistant under Dr. James Simpson at Edinburgh University. He was one of the best surgeons in the world. It was he who had first used chloroform as a means of relieving pain. A daring act for him to take a woman as his assistant. It was a position any young male doctor just out of medical school might well have envied—and did! But Emily was not any young doctor, as Elizabeth well knew. She had robust health, abundant energy, a fine mind, and a wonderful memory. She was trained not only in medicine but in mathematics, Greek, Latin, German, and French. Dr. Simpson seemed to enjoy shocking his colleagues, as one incident Emily wrote about proved.

Once when his office was filled with patients, some of them lords and ladies, Emily was doing some translating for him in an inner room.

"Dr. Blackwell," he called to her in a low voice, then he spoke a little louder. "Dr. Blackwell!" To make sure that all his patients heard and were watching, he thundered, "DR. BLACKWELL!" Then he watched with amusement the expressions on his patients' faces when they saw a *woman* come through the door.

But Emily was far away, and meanwhile Elizabeth was struggling with almost impossible tasks and worries alone.

Then one morning she woke and smelled the sea. Her spirits rose like a soaring gull. It might mean a storm was coming, but for her it meant renewed strength. With the tang of the sea in her nostrils, she could do anything. And something wonderful, she felt, was going to happen. Something did.

The doorbell rang. A woman stood on the stoop. Except for her eyes, dark and intelligent under heavy black brows, she was almost homely.

"Dok-tor Black-well?" Elizabeth had many German patients, and she recognized the accent.

"Yes," she replied in her very poor German. "Can I help you?"

The woman burst into a volley of German, out of which Elizabeth caught one name, Miss Goodrich, matron of a home for the friendless.

"Oh, yes," she said. "Miss Goodrich told me about you. You are Fraulein—"

"I—Marie Zakrsewska."

The name was not so hard to pronounce, after all, the way she said it. Zak-shef-ska.

Marie had come to America from Germany hoping to study medicine. She had been a head midwife in a hospital in Berlin, but when the kind director had died, she had been ousted because she was a woman. Reading her credentials, Elizabeth was amazed. This woman had held one of the most distinguished positions in a great Berlin hospital! She had been chief midwife, head professor in the School of Midwives, the largest hospital in Prussia. No wonder after the death of her friend, her male associates had managed to get rid of her!

That summer Elizabeth was no longer lonely. She became Marie's instructor, and tried to teach her English. But that proved almost hopeless. Her brilliance did not extend to language! However, with her German she was of wonderful assistance in the dispensary.

All that summer, while the thermometer sometimes reached 102, Elizabeth tramped in her long skirts through the dusty streets, carrying her black doctor's sack, and sweating inside her petticoats and corsets. She gave free service in the dispensary, often unthanked. She delivered babies in reeking and stifling tenements. But with Marie to help her, always cheerful, eager to learn, there was at least no loneliness.

However, Marie must not stay. For months Elizabeth worked to get her into a good medical school, and at last she secured her admission to the Cleveland Medical College, where Emily had graduated. Elizabeth sent her off on October 16, 1854 with medical textbooks, twenty dollars to cover travel and fees, and exactly thirty dollars for all other expenses.

In spite of her delight over Marie's good fortune, Elizabeth had never been more discouraged or lonely. The dispensary was not doing as well as she had hoped. The people who had backed it were losing their enthusiasm. Pledges had not been paid. Patients forgot the hours and failed to come. Closed so much of the time, the room was chilly and damp. Must she close it entirely before winter? Yet how desperately it was needed, not just one small room six hours a week, but a real full-time dispensary!

Even her family seemed to be deserting her. Anna was trying to persuade Emily to settle in England. Harry was going on a journey in pursuit of this new love of his. Marian, who had been living near New York, was planning to return to Cincinnati for the winter. Her dream of a house for the family was fading. The long cold winter ahead looked desolate. Would all her coming years be like this, everybody seeming to run off and leave her, no one who really belonged to her?

One day those words of Emily's came back to her. "Why don't you take a little orphan girl—" She didn't like the idea at first. Too many women she knew had taken orphans just to get free help, making little slaves of them. And yet— if one did it for the right reasons—

"I'll do it," she decided suddenly.

It was a decision that was to change her life.

15

THE ARRIVAL OF KITTY

At Randall's Island, where immigrant orphans were held, Elizabeth was shown handsome, healthy children. She listened to their histories and habits, and was even shown their gums and teeth.

Like a horse trader, she thought.

Her eyes kept returning to a child standing by the window, hands clasped behind, with her eyes fixed on the glowing sunset. She was not pretty. Her face was sharp and thin. Her arms and legs were like pipestems and her hair was so jet black and riotous that it gave her a witchlike look.

"Tell me about that child there," she said to the matron, "the one looking out the window."

The matron looked shocked. "Oh, but you wouldn't want her. She's a good little thing, but plain, as you can see, and quite stupid. Now this one here—"

"I'd like to know more about her," insisted Elizabeth.

The matron knew little about the child, only that she was between seven and eight, was Irish, an orphan, with no living soul to claim her. Even her name, Katharine Barry, was doubtful.

Marian, who had come with Elizabeth, was dismayed. "Not *her*, Bessie!"

"Why not?" demanded Elizabeth. "Look at her. She's been fairly drinking in that sunset."

Marian was indignant. "She— she's almost ugly! And weak and pindling. I thought you were looking for a strong, intelligent child you could train to help you."

"I thought so too," Elizabeth answered. "But this child needs me more than any of the others."

She went to the window and took one of the child's small hands. "Would you like to go home with me, dear, and be my little girl?"

The eyes that lifted to look at her were bright and clear. "Yes. But could we please wait until the colors fade?" Elizabeth dropped to her knees before the window, and together they watched until the brightness faded to a pale yellow glow. It was an experience of sharing that was to be repeated again and again, over half a century.

"No difficulty was made," Elizabeth wrote Emily. "I gave a receipt for her, and the poor little thing followed behind me. Instead of being stupid, I have found that now she is withdrawn from blows and tyranny, she is very bright, has able little fingers that are learning to dust and wash up and sew with much perseverance, and lots of energy for so small a child. She is a sturdy little thing, affectionate, and with a touch of obstinacy that will turn to good account later in life. Of course, she is more trouble than use at present and quite bewildered me at first, but still I like on the whole having her, and it is a joy to hear her in the morning, sitting up in bed, waiting for permission to get up and singing, 'Oh, Susanna, don't you cry for me, I'm going to Alabama with me washboard on me knee.' She is not pretty but has an honest little face, and it is growing brighter every day. So you can imagine me now, attended by small Kitty, attired in my colored Paris straw bonnet, and a black silk cape of mine that hangs over her like a mantle."

A little servant? Hardly! Elizabeth knew that on the very first night when she carried the small thin body up to bed in her arms. Even then her feeling was not that of a mistress toward a servant, but of mother toward daughter.

Slowly the thin body rounded, the stooped shoulders straightened. Elizabeth was determined to give Kitty every advantage. She enrolled her in one of the best schools in the city. When the streets were banked by deep snows, she would tuck the child under her arm and carry her over the long crossing, from the corner of Fifteenth street, across the end of Union Square, to the corner of Fourteenth and Broadway. From there Kitty could walk down two streets to the school. Then, even though it meant closing the office early in the afternoon, she would go to get her in the evenings.

Far from being stupid, Kitty proved to be very bright. She noticed things.

"You'd better pay attention to what that child says about clothes," advised Marian, who had always taken a dim view of Elizabeth's taste in dress. "Her eyes are sharp and keen."

And they were keen to notice other things.

"Your hands," Kitty said once to Elizabeth, lifting one of them to her cheek. "They're beautiful. Such long fingers. And they're cool to feel, but not—not moist. And I like the way you always warm them before you touch a sick person. It must keep them from being frightened, especially the babies."

"You noticed that!" exclaimed Elizabeth, surprised.

At first the child did not call her Aunt Elizabth or Aunt Bessie, as she often did later, but Doctor or My Doctor. Once she happened to be in the room during the visit of one of Elizabeth's friends, another physician.

"Doctor," she said after the man had gone, "how very odd it is to hear a *man* called Doctor!"

It was the beginning of a new contentment for Elizabeth. She was no longer lonely, and for the first time she felt a uniting of two conflicting desires in her nature—her career as a doctor and motherhood.

16

OTHER DREAMS COME TRUE

The dispensary did indeed have to close that winter, but with Elizabeth's prodding her supporters raised more money, and it opened in even better quarters. By the end of February, 1855, two hundred poor women had received treatment. But Elizabeth was far from satisfied. She must have a hospital! However, that meant raising at least five thousand dollars, a huge sum in those days. How to do it?

She wished she could be as successful as her brother Harry in reaching the desired goal. For Harry had at last persuaded his reluctant Lucy to become his wife. Elizabeth still did not approve of his choice, but—could she be wrong? After all, she had only seen Lucy speaking from a platform, organizing and running noisy women's rights conventions, and being hooted at in the streets for wearing bloomers. Yet often she had been hooted at in the streets! Could it be that she had doubts just because she and Lucy were so much alike?

Elizabeth could not go to the wedding, but she wrote Lucy a cordial letter, all the while telling herself that she might have been wrong. She had been, for the marriage was to be one of the happiest in history. Like some other women far in the future, Lucy refused to take her husband's name, remaining all her life Lucy Stone. In fact, women who were to follow her example would often be called Lucy Stoners.

"Silly," thought Elizabeth, "refusing to use the name of the man you had chosen, preferring that of a father you had *not* chosen!"

Less than a year later Sam was married to his love, Antoinette Brown. The Blackwells were certainly in the forefront of daring pioneers. And Elizabeth was one of them. With the coming of a new year her hopes began to soar.

"My thirty-fifth birthday," she wrote in her journal on February 2, 1856. "I feel full of hope and strength for the future. Kitty plays beside me with her doll. Who will ever guess the help that little orphan has been to me!"

And when Marie— Dr. Zak—came back with her medical degree, buoyant with energy, hope became even stronger.

"Von year from dis day yoost," Marie vowed in her slowly improving English, "ve open our new hospital, *ja?*"

Elizabeth caught her breath. A hospital by May, 1857? It seemed like an impossible dream. The house had been chosen, yes, the old Roosevelt building on Bleecker Street. She had an option on it. However, it would take not just five thousand dollars, but ten! May as well dream of a million! But, listening to Marie, so young, so hopeful, anything seemed possible.

"*Ja!*" she agreed recklessly.

If the hospital were to become reality, Marie realized, she must help raise the money. They could rent the Roosevelt house for thirteen hundred dollars a year. Marie went to Boston and returned with pledges of six hundred and fifty dollars. Joyfully she and Elizabeth set out to raise the rest. But they met a storm of protest.

"What if people die in your hospital?" some would demand. "Your death certificates would not be recognized."

"Without men doctors, how could you control the patients?"

At least one of Elizabeth's dreams was coming true. That year Sam and Harry, with their wives, and their mother Hannah, moved into Elizabeth's big house on Fifteenth Street. At last she had her family around her.

Kitty was entranced. She liked having a big family, as well as her "Doctor." There was a sweet-faced grandmother with bright eyes and pink cheeks, white curls peeping from the edges of her cap, aunts and uncles, and, best of all, a baby was on the way. She was on her way to bed when she met Dr. Zak coming down the stairs.

Antoinette had had a baby girl. She was named Florence, like hundreds of other new arrivals, after Florence Nightingale. After taking her band of women to the Crimea to nurse sick soldiers, she was known all over the world as the Lady of the Lamp.

"Vould you like to see a baby?" asked the doctor, smiling.

"Oh—yes!" Kitty knew that both her doctors had the remarkable ability of helping to produce babies, but never before had it happened here. "Where is it? Where did it come from?"

"In big room upstairs. And it came out of a— a cabbage."

Kitty gave her a scornful glance and said, "Nothing so nice as a baby ever came out of a cabbage!" She rushed upstairs. There on a large pillow before an open fire lay the new arrival, very tiny indeed.

"Don't step on my baby!" cried Uncle Sam jovially.

Grandma taught Kitty how to hold the baby, very carefully, to support its back, and after that the two of them carried it out on every fair day for a walk in the sunshine. Kitty mourned when Uncle Sam, who now had a good job in the city, took Aunt Nette and Florence and moved over to Newark, where they lived in a tall slim house that Uncle Harry dubbed the Pepper Box.

Elizabeth loved having her house full. And with everybody helping with expenses, she was able to reduce her mortgage. Surely now her dream of a hospital must come true. It all depended on a fair planned for December. Women supporters had been sewing furiously, and Philadelphia and Boston friends sent contributions. But no church or public building would give them space! Finally one of the Quaker women loaned an unfinished loft. She provided a crystal chandelier and other women loaned rugs and draperies. Horace Greeley gave them good publicity in his paper. Wonderful! People came. They actually raised the six hundred dollars needed. She could have her hospital—at least for one year.

She called it the New York Infirmary for Women and Children, and it was opened on May 12, 1857, Florence Nightingale's birthday. They had actually accomplished it in the year planned. It seemed a miracle to Elizabeth. Emily came back from Europe in time for the great opening.

Guests came, filling the space in the surrounding streets with carriages. The women wore billowing skirts and carried ruffled parasols. The men were dressed in morning coats and top hats. Henry Ward Beecher gave the main address.

Elizabeth told them what the infirmary's tasks would be, providing women physicians, training women medical students, and training nurses, three things seldom before attempted by any institution in the country.

"Women," she said, "must prove their medical ability before they can expect to be recognized by the medical profession."

The lower floor was the dispensary. The second floor held two six-bed wards, and the third floor was the maternity department for mothers and new babies. In the big attic there were two large and two small rooms, living quarters for the doctors, servants, and—did Elizabeth dare hope for it?—four or five medical students. All the rooms would be heated by open fireplaces.

There! It was finished . . . and begun. With the sign boldly fastened to the front door, the three doctors sat down to wait, but not for long. Soon people came, some of the patients from the old Tompkins Square dispensary, awed at first by the more stylish neighborhood, but reassured by the familiar faces. They brought others.

Before a month passed the six-bed wards were filled, and there was a daily attendance of thirty or more. Elizabeth was the director, Emily the surgeon, Marie the resident physician, superintendent, and housekeeper. To Elizabeth's delight, two girls came for nurses' training. So the New York Infirmary became the first school of nursing in America.

Dr. Zak had the biggest job, which she shouldered with her usual energy and cheerfulness. At 5:30 in the morning she started out in an omnibus for the market to buy supplies, and at eight she was back for breakfast. For everybody except patients, breakfast consisted of tea, bread and butter, mush meal, and syrup. On Sundays coffee and bacon were added. After breakfast she visited patients in the house, while Elizabeth and Emily treated those in the dispensary. Then Marie took another omnibus trip to the druggist's, begging and buying the needed supplies. She arrived home in time for the one o'clock dinner, which consisted of soup, soup meat, potatoes, one vegetable, and fruit. On Sundays there would be a roast or steak.

After dinner all the doctors attended their private patients, who were their chief means of support. The four dollars charged to paying hospital patients were barely enough to cover the cost of medical service. Money was scarce, and most of their house visits were among the poor who could not afford to pay.

One night in a Negro quarter, they entered a tiny sweltering room filled with people, faces shading from pitch black to one almost white. Their patient was lying in one corner. On a table stood a small smoky lamp. At least eight of the children belonged to the patient, and there must have been a dozen others. After delivering the little mulatto baby, the doctors went home through the dark streets at one in the morning. Such an experience was typical.

There was still opposition because they were women doctors. In spite of Elizabeth's insistence on cleanliness and sanitation, fever sometimes developed after a childbirth. One woman died of it. An hour after it occurred Elizabeth was startled by a loud commotion in the street outside. She rushed to the door. A crowd was yelling in the street. She saw raised fists, hoes and shovels, and threatening faces. She recognized some of the dead patient's relatives, sisters, aunts, and cousins, who had watched by her bedside. They must have rounded up all their male relatives and neighbors!

"You killed her, you killed her!" she heard a woman scream. As she leaned against the door she could feel it shaking, they continued to beat and pound. She heard other shouts.

"You in there! Women doctors!" . . . "Not doctors, killers!" . . . "Kill women, that's what you do!" . . . "We'll show you what we do to murderers!"

Marie appeared, dark eyes burning in her white face. "Dey're filling de yard. I've locked all dors, but ve can't hold out long. Vat— vat ve do?"

Elizabeth pressed so hard against the door that her knuckles showed white, but her face stayed calm. "Perhaps I should go out and talk to them—"

"No! Dey kill you! Did you see faces—like beasts!"

Elizabeth peered through one of the window panes. To her horror she saw a big workman coming toward the front steps carrying a crowbar. She must stop him, open the door before he broke it down. Then suddenly she recognized him. It was an Irish workman whose wife had been treated at the old dispensary. Pushing his way through the crowd, he mounted the steps.

"You there! By the saints in heaven, what the divil's goin' on? What do you think you doin'?"

The noise subsided, then rose again as all the relatives tried to explain at once.

"Quiet! Saints help us, one at a time!" Finally he got the story. "I see. Your woman had a baby, and she died. So what? Lots of women die when babies are born. What's all this hullabaloo?"

The noise swelled. "Women doctors— killed her—"

"Quiet!" His voice boomed. "Now you listen to me. I know these doctors, and lots of you know them too. My wife had pneumony, and they made her well, same as they've made lots of you well. I ask you what've other doctors ever done for you, give yer medicines, go into yer lousy houses, care whether you live or dies? Saints help us, ain't you got no brains? Doctors ain't God. Don't you know there ain't no doctor what could keep everybody from dyin' when they gets sick?"

Heads nodded sheepishly. The crowd stopped being a mob, and became just a group of curious and worried human beings. Finally they went away.

"It's all right," Elizabeth told the relatives later when they tried to apologize. "You could not help yourselves. Women doctors have to prove themselves."

There were some bold men doctors who helped them by acting as consultants in spite of the sneers and frowns of their colleagues. Some of them found to their surprise that the women could teach them new ideas. In the big city dispensaries no records were kept. To their amazement they learned that at Elizabeth's dispensary every patient could be traced—name, residence, diagnosis, treament, result—and that no doctor or student was permitted to give a prescription without signing her name. They could hardly believe it.

There were a few medical students as well as those studying nursing. Some came to work in the summer from their classes at the new Philadelphia Women's Medical College. Thanks to Elizabeth's ideas of hygiene, the students became missionaries as well as healers. Sponges, soap and medicines were carried in their satchels and given out with talks on cleanliness. Even more unheard of than the keeping of records were the ideas that sick people should be bathed and kept clean, and that fresh air does not kill. Both cleanliness and ventilation might even prevent sickness. Elizabeth was at least fifty years ahead of her time!

17

KITTY AND HER FAMILY

Instead of having no relatives at all, Kitty now had a bewildering number. They kept coming and going in the big Fifteenth Street house. After Uncle Sam, Aunt Nette, and little Florence were gone, there were still Uncle Harry and Aunt Lucy, but for some reason her name wasn't Blackwell but Stone. She was away a lot lecturing about something called women's rights, and Uncle Harry was trying to find work. Finally he got a job with a firm publishing books, and to Kitty's disappointment they also moved away to a cottage in New Jersey.

She was even more disappointed when Dr. Emily returned one day in the fall with her little black doctor's bag and the news that Uncle Harry and Aunt Lucy had a baby. Surely they could have arranged to have it at Fifteenth Street! Kitty was sure now that cabbages had little or nothing to do with babies. Now she suspected that they came somehow from the doctors' little black bags. Once when Elizabeth was going out on a baby case she managed to peek into the black bag, but to her disappointment there was no baby in it.

There was great discussion over the new baby's name. Should it be Stone or Blackwell? At last they decided on both names. They thought about Sarah, but Aunt Ellen, whom Kitty had never seen, wrote that she had been christened Sarah Ellen and had dropped the first name because she didn't like it. Finally they settled on Alice, Alice Stone Blackwell. Gazing at the red-faced mite with all her baby-loving enthusiasm, Kitty little knew how, next to her beloved Doctor, this young cousin was to become the great love and bosom friend of her life.

Kitty was as much a member of the family now as any of the Blackwells. When one of My Doctor's friends came from England to visit, she was proud to be introduced as "my dear little daughter-niece." But one day when she overheard them talking, her heart almost stopped beating.

"Please, Elizabeth, you must come back to England, if only for a visit. Women there have made no progress in medicine compared with here. You have hosts of friends there. We can arrange lectures for you. Please— won't you come?"

"But— how could I leave here?"

"With two other doctors? Of course you could. Promise you'll think about it."

Kitty waited tensely for the answer. "I promise," said Elizabeth slowly.

Kitty felt cold all over. If My Doctor went to England, what would become of her? Would she be farmed out to other members of the family? But some, she knew, had not approved of My Doctor's taking her. Stashed at the infirmary? Horrible thought. She liked Dr. Zak, but Rosalia, Dr. Zak's sister, was there, and once Rosalia had locked Kitty in the bedroom, telling her she must stay there until she said she hated Dr. Blackwell. "Hate My Doctor!" Kitty had spouted indignantly, and had remained locked up until Dr. Zak discovered the locked door and let her out. And suppose My Doctor liked England so well that she never came back! Would Kitty be sent back to the orphanage?

But months passed, and she almost forgot the horrible possibility. Then came spring, and she overheard more conversation.

". . . Only be gone a few months . . . Sure you and Dr. Zak can manage? . . . They do seem to need me . . ."

Sudden excitement postponed her fear when My Doctor left with her little black bag for New Jersey. There was sadness when she returned, for Aunt Nette, it seemed, had had another baby, and it had died. For some time the word "England" was not even mentioned.

Then the awful moment came. The coldness in her small body was like ice.

"Kitty, dear, I have decided to go to England, not for long, just a visit. I hope you will be happy about it. You know I want you to be happy."

"Yes." The ice in her throat made it sound like a croak.

"We haven't long to get ready. We must begin preparations at once."

"We?" The word exploded in an upsurge of wild hope.

My Doctor looked surprised. "Why— yes, dear. You're going with me."

They sailed in August on a ship named *Persia,* a combination of sails and steam. Even seasickness did not spoil Kitty's enjoyment. She promenaded the long decks with My Doctor and Captain Judkins. She lay in a deck chair and watched the billowing sails. At night she loved to hear the watchman call out, "All's well ahead!" and hear the cry pass from prow to middle watch to stern.

In England she met more Blackwells, Uncle Howard, burned brown from having just been in India, and Aunt Ellen, who had been studying art in France and England. And here the wonderful enjoyment ended, for she was sent to boarding school, a very modern school for both girls and boys.

Kitty hated the school. She hated everything about it.

"How well you speak English!" one of the pupils said in surprise.

"What should I speak?" retorted Kitty in disgust. Did they think America was peopled by Hottentots?

She hated the discipline, the food, the senseless English manners. If you came late for breakfast or prayers, you might be sent to bed for a whole day. All the other pupils were fond of a pudding called treacle, with bottom, side, and top crusts as thick as boards, and the inside filled with syrup. She loathed it. She despised having to make curtsies to the ladies and gentlemen they met on walks. One day she was in the park, playing games with a boy about her age. She told him indignantly that he was cheating. His nurse told her that was no way to speak to his lordship. Why not? She knew nothing about lords, but she knew well enough when somebody was not playing fair.

My Doctor was in France. She had given Kitty stamped envelopes to write her in case of emergency. Well— wasn't being unhappy an emergency? She wrote an appealing letter, and action was prompt. Her prison term was over! She was to go and stay with Aunt Ellen. Then, when word came that she was to go to Paris, her joy was complete.

But there were difficulties. She must have a passport. Charles Francis Adams, the American minister, and Mr. Moran, his chief, both said it was impossible to give a child a passport. Uncle Howie took her to the passport office many times.

"Now, Kitty," he said, "if they say this time they will give it to you, you must take off your right-hand glove when they give you the book, to swear."

Success! They had decided to give it. "Little girl," said Mr. Adams in his deep voice, "do you understand the nature of an oath?"

"Yes, sir," she replied. "It's to tell the truth and nothing but the truth."

They gave her the passport. Fourteen years later, when she went to the same office for another passport, Mr. Moran was still there. Being told who she was, he said, "We never did such a thing before or since, and if anything had happened to you, the United States Embassy would never have heard the last of it."

One dark morning Uncle Howie roused her at an unearthly hour and took her to Waterloo Station. In one pocket of her cape was the passport; in the other were the addresses in Paris and Dieppe where she would have to stop. Arriving at Newhaven, she followed the stream of people aboard the boat. She sat down on a bench and watched all the preparations for starting. When they were out of the harbor, a sailor came and asked if she would not go below to the cabin. She went to the head of the stairway, but did not like the smell.

"No, thank you," she told him with dignity. "I will stay here."

He carefully wrapped her in tarpaulins, yet when she arrived at Dieppe in France she looked

like a drowned rat, wet from her swansdown hood
to the bottom of her cape. She marched off the
boat between a file of soldiers and a curious
crowd. As they neared the Custom House, a lady
approached her. It was one of Aunt Anna's
friends.

At her flat the maid carried off her clothes to
dry and press. Kitty knew enough French to thank
her. Again she was put on a train, reaching Paris
at two in the morning. No one was there to meet
her.

After her trunk was examined, there was a great
crowd of porters and officials, all looking
curiously at her. She showed the address given
her to the station master, asked for a cab to go
there, and presently was deposited in one. All the
officials regarded with obvious alarm the sight of a
small, black-eyed, black-haired youngster driving
off alone.

Kitty also was alarmed. She had read too many
stories of the French Revolution. She fully expected to be carried to the Bastille or some other
prison. When the cab suddenly stopped she
thought the hour had come. Looking out, she saw
another cab coming in the opposite direction.

"Is that you, child?" asked a familiar voice.

Elizabeth was far more relieved than Kitty. She
had gone to the wrong station. When she reached
the right one, Kitty had gone, but all the officials
there had been able to give her information. Now,
riding along she had recognized Kitty's small
trunk on top of another cab and stopped her own.
Never would she forget the sight of the little
dead-white face with its frightened black eyes and
frame of jet-black hair.

Another relative, a woman with a beautiful face,
but restless eyes and thin lips, was waiting at the

house, Aunt Anna. She had a small apartment with a lovely sheep's fur rug on the floor and a bright fire in the grate. Eating a good lunch and, afterward, tumbling into a nice soft bed, Kitty sank into drowsy comfort. But it was none of these things that made it all seem like heaven. It was just being with My Doctor again. The country, the surroundings, the time did not matter. She had come home.

18

CLOUDS OF WAR

Decisions, decisions! Elizabeth was bombarded with them. She felt as bewildered as when she and Kitty had walked through the fogs in Paris, groping their way along and feeling delighted when they ran into a policeman. Should she stay here in Europe or go back to America?

Florence Nightingale had asked her to visit. Elizabeth was shocked at the sight of her. She lay on a couch, bolstered by pillows, a mere shell of her former self. Except for her eyes! They were blazing fires. She had spent all her strength in nursing soldiers in the Crimean War. But she was still full of energy.

"Hospitals!" she exclaimed scornfully. "I have visited them, and they are shocking. Damp walls, dirty floors and beds, no sanitation, poor food, wretched nursing. I must do something to change them, and you must help me. I want to found a school for women nurses. I will be the organizer, and you will be the director. Except for the one where I trained in Germany, it will be the first women's nursing school in the world."

Elizabeth did not correct her, though she had been running a school for women nurses in New York for several years.

"Don't give me an answer now." As Elizabeth hesitated, Florence lifted a small hand. "Take time. Make up your mind as to whether you can give up America. I know it is a serious matter."

It certainly was serious. But it was not her only problem. A wealthy countess whom she met wanted her to found a hospital for women in London and promised five thousand pounds toward the project. And many other important people were urging her to remain—George Eliot, the writer; Lady Byron, widow of the famous poet; and of course the countess. She was tempted.

Already she was accomplishing much. She gave a series of lectures in one of London's big halls, and their success exceeded her wildest dreams. People listened eagerly. Mothers begged her for instruction in health. Three young women said they wanted to become medical students.

But her greatest triumph was yet to come. She was determined that the name of a woman should be included in the new Medical Register of Great Britain. On the Medical Council were some of her friends. She submitted some of her records and made application. Success would be a major achievement for women doctors. And to her delight it came.

"I have only one piece of information to send," she wrote Emily jubilantly in June, 1859. "The Medical Council has registered me as a physician!"

How great a triumph it was even she did not realize. Hastily the council made it impossible for another woman to repeat the honor, and it would be many years before women doctors received such recognition.

Remain in England? Her first enthusiasm cooled. Florence Nightingale was not interested in women becoming doctors, only nurses. The countess proved unpredictable. Give up the sure, if small, beginning in America for vague promises? No. In the summer of 1859 she and Kitty crossed the ocean again.

New York had changed. It was full of unrest. Wherever she went Elizabeth saw worried black faces, and heard hot arguments. Tension and fear were spreading all over the country. For Elizabeth the trouble had one cause: slavery.

But she had other things to worry her, especially Emily. Her sister's cheeks were gaunt. Her shoulders drooped.

"What have you been doing to yourself, Milly?" she reproached her.

But she knew very well what Emily had been doing. Dr. Zak had left to start a women's medical college in Boston. Emily had had the whole responsibility of the infirmary. She had had to struggle with poverty. While Elizabeth had been entertained lavishly by friends in England, Emily had been living in her garret, keeping in a bureau drawer bread, oranges, dates, and a few other simple foods. Sometimes she cooked a little meat over an alcohol lamp or took a small leg of lamb to the infirmary for roasting. Elizabeth was conscience stricken.

But the infirmary had prospered, and Elizabeth knew it was time to enlarge the work again. Already they had been training a few medical students along with the nurses. But they should have a real medical school. It meant finding a new building. She did find a suitable one at the corner of Eighth Street and Second Avenue, and she persuaded the trustees to buy it.

"Why not sell our house?" suggested Emily. "We

could move into the infirmary. It would reduce both work and expense."

Reluctantly Elizabeth did so. Gone was her dream of having a place for the whole family to come, live, and visit! She, Kitty, and Emily moved into the new building. They slept in the garret, cooked and ate in the basement, but the new roomy wards and dispensary made it all worthwhile.

Then came a blow.

"I think I will give up medicine," said Emily one day.

Elizabeth stared at her. "You— what?"

"I've been thinking about it a long time. Maybe I made a mistake studying medicine in the first place."

Elizabeth felt as if she were in a bad dream.

"Milly, you can't mean that! You're a wonderful doctor! Your patients worship you ..." The words trailed off.

"Yes," said Emily, "I am a good doctor. But I might have been good at something else, too. Maybe art, like Ellen."

Elizabeth was stunned. It was because of her that Emily had decided to be a doctor. Had she been trying to create a replica of herself rather than encourage the fulfillment of another person?

"Milly," she said humbly, "what would you like to do?"

"I'm not sure. Perhaps study art. Anyway, it won't be for a long time. I must save money first. I won't desert your work yet."

She had said "your" work, not "ours."

"I'll help, Milly, dear," Elizabeth said gently. "We're making a little money now. We'll make more. We'll make your dream come true, and soon."

But it would not be soon, for already clouds of war were forming. And the storm soon came. In April, 1861, the first shot was fired at Fort Sumter, and soon men were on the march toward Washington.

The smoke had scarcely cleared at Fort Sumter when Elizabeth said to Emily, "Do you realize, Milly, that the infirmary is the only place in the country where nurses are being trained. They are going to need nurses, well-trained ones."

"Yes," said Emily. "And I know exactly what you're thinking."

Elizabeth called a meeting of some of their women friends at the infirmary. So many came that a public meeting was called at Cooper Institute, where Abraham Lincoln had addressed a similar big crowd before he was elected president. Between three and four thousand women came. They organized a Women's Central Association of Relief. But the army refused their help. War, said the officer in charge in New York, was soldiers' business, and civilians had no right to meddle. Certainly not women, he might have added.

But the women were as obstinate as Florence Nightingale had been in facing the same opposition. It was a long battle, but finally they won. The American Sanitary Commission was formed, forerunner of the American Red Cross.

Elizabeth's task was to examine candidates for nursing, then send them to be trained at the infirmary before a month of further training in New York hospitals. Short as this training was, it was far more than most army nurses were getting. Dorothea Dix, superintendent of nurses in Washington, had simple requirements for admission—only that candidates should be at least thirty, plain of feature, and severely dressed in brown or black.

Neither training nor experience was necessary. She felt that the morals of the soldiers were more important than their health.

The months rushed past. During 1862 the infirmary treated nearly seven thousand patients. Many were black refugees from the South. If Elizabeth and Emily had had enemies because they were women, they now had even more. Many people were tired of the war, and they blamed the Negroes for it.

It was in July, 1863, that excitement flared white-hot. Elizabeth and Kitty had been taking a needed holiday with the family in New Jersey.

"Riots are blazing in the city," they heard one evening. "You mustn't go back."

"Of course, we must go," returned Elizabeth calmly, "and at once. If there's trouble, we'll be needed more than ever."

Crossing the Hudson by ferry they saw the city skyline lurid with fire. Arriving on the other side, they took a cab. Elizabeth felt as if she were back in Bristol riots of her childhood. The figures she glimpsed under the dim lights looked the same—upraised fists carrying brickbats and crowbars; faces inflamed with a wild excitement. Occasionally there was a crash of glass, as one shop after another was broken into and looted.

As they neared the infirmary, closer to the Negro and immigrant sections, it became worse. Here homes were being fired and battered down. Suddenly Elizabeth put her arm about Kitty, pressing the girl's face hard against her shoulder. But she was too late. Kitty had already seen the limp, black-faced figure dangling from a lamppost.

Emily met them at the door. "Thank heaven, you've come! The white patients are demanding that we oust the black women. Of course, I told them we wouldn't."

So began three days and nights of horror. The second night was the worst. The rioters burned eleven houses only a block away from the infirmary. Elizabeth was sick at heart. If the infimary were destroyed, she knew it would never be rebuilt, for Emily would be leaving. How could she ever find courage to begin all over again?

The night was half over when Elizabeth was called to the tiny delivery room, where Emily was bent over a refugee slave brought to the infirmary by friends. The woman was near starvation and exhausted by the terrors of her escape. Quickly Elizabeth changed into a clean white sack and washed her hands in disinfectant. All the rest of the night the three women labored. Only when the baby was safely born, washed, oiled, laid in its basket, the young mother back in her bed, eyes radiant with a son born into freedom, did the two doctors relax. Then, very tired, they exchanged smiles of satisfaction. Not begin again? Of course she would.

Elizabeth was surprised to find that day had come. The doors and windows were still intact, the fires a block away. Though the riots raged for another day and night, the infirmary remained untouched.

The war crawled on, and Elizabeth continued to examine and train nurses, working almost day and night. Then one day in June, because of the contribution she had made, she was invited to go to Washington.

"It's about time," Emily sputtered. "They should have recognized all the work you've been doing ages ago!"

Elizabeth was to make an inspection tour of the

Nursing Corps, but it was a holiday as well as a business trip. One of its greatest pleasures was in meeting her old Philadelphia friend, Dr. Elder, who had an office in one of the government buildings. He took her to the new Capitol, which at President Lincoln's inauguration had been just "blocks of marble and iron castings," but which was now complete even to its majestic dome. She walked miles, seeing the Washington Monument, the Library of Congress, the Senate and House rooms. But the sight of tents and baggage trains, of wagons bringing wounded soldiers from the wharves, of disabled men in the lobby of her hotel, spoiled all the joy of holiday.

The high point of the trip came when, with Dr. Elder, she visited the president's house. As they were leaving, Judge Kelly of Philadelphia met them.

"Why don't you go up and see the president?" he asked. "He's all alone."

So up they went. Kelly opened the door of a large square room on the second floor, announced "Dr. Elder and Miss Blackwell of New York," and left.

"A tall, ungainly, loose-jointed man was standing in the middle of the room," Elizabeth wrote Kitty. "He came forward with a pleasant smile and shook hands with us. I should not have recognized him from the photographs. He is much uglier than any I have seen."

"Miss Blackwell," explained Dr. Elder in the course of their conversation, "was the second woman to become a citizen of the United States by naturalization."

Elizabeth smiled. "But I believe Queen Victoria reserved the privilege of shooting me."

"Yes." The responding smile lit the craggy face

like a burst of sunlight. "That was the chief cause, I believe, of our War of 1812."

"Then," Elizabeth continued in writing Kitty, "he plumped his long body down on a corner of the large table that stood in the center of the room, caught up one knee, and began to discuss some point about the war. A fat clerk came into the room with papers and stood fidgeting, evidently wishing us out of the way, so, of course, we said good morning. Altogether it was a most characteristic little peep, much better than any parade glimpse, so I considered myself quite in luck."

She little realized that within months, amid her rejoicing over the end of the war, she would be lamenting with a shocked nation the death of this strange and lonely leader who, as she wrote a friend in England, "expressed the American heartbeat."

19

"CHILDREN ARE BORN TO LIVE"

The war had ended. But for many war was just beginning, like the newly freed slaves who were yet to face long battles with poverty and prejudice. For women, who had proved they could become leaders in life outside their homes, but still had almost no legal rights, and could not even vote. For Elizabeth.

She still had not realized her dream of establishing a women's medical college, and it seemed next to impossible. But in 1866, the year after the war ended, she was able to realize another dream.

"Children are born to live, not die," she was constantly saying.

She appointed a woman known as a sanitary visitor, whose only work was to go into the homes of poor people in the neighborhood and try to prevent, not just treat, sickness. She would talk to the mothers about fresh air, cleanliness, warmth, healthy food, and clothing. Sometimes she would teach them how to cook with foods that were cheap yet nourishing. She would show them how to air their bedding and open windows without getting drafts. She would help find work for those who needed it. And she would make careful reports of every home visited.

"Mary G," they might read, "5 children, 4 dead, 1 sick; Mary K., 2 children, 1 dead, 1 sick; Ann H., 7 children, 5 dead, 2 sick; Catherine W., 10 children, 5 dead . . ."

Nobody had ever heard of such work before. It would be at least forty years before New York or any other city would start such a visiting nursing service. Most doctors made fun of it. As if cleanliness or fresh air or proper food had anything to do with sickness!

One of these first visitors was Dr. Rebecca Cole, who had graduated from the Woman's Medical College of Pennsylvania. She was one of the first black women ever to become a doctor. During the nine years that she worked, over ten thousand visits were made.

But the medical college. Would it ever come? If Emily decided to leave, as she had once suggested, how could Elizabeth fulfill her dream alone? Suddenly she was faced with that very prospect. News came of their brother Howard's death.

"Oh, poor Anna!" they both exclaimed.

For Howie had been their sister Anna's idol. Her dream had been to make a home for him somewhere, if he ever decided to stay in one place long enough. Anna was still in Paris, writing, lonely, never quite attaining happiness.

"One of us must go to her," said Elizabeth. "You or I or Marian."

"Not I," replied Emily. "You forget. There are ten years between us, and Anna and I were never close. Besides, my place is here."

Elizabeth tensed. For five years, it seemed, she had been waiting for this moment.

"Milly," she said quietly, "this could be your chance."

Emily looked puzzled. "Chance for what?"

"To get away. Give up medicine. Study art, travel. The things you said you wanted to do. Think of it— Paris, the art center of the world. You could—"

She stopped, surprised by Emily's look of astonishment.

"What an idea! Why on earth should I want to go to Paris and study art?"

"B-but— you said— surely you remember—"

"One says many things. Besides, that was five years ago."

"Then you mean—you're no longer planning to— to give up medicine?"

"I'm forty years old," said Emily calmly. "I spent many long years learning to be a doctor. No one knows that better than you. It would be stupid to think of other work now. Besides, I'm needed here."

It was Elizabeth who went abroad that summer. Kitty did not go. She was going with Henry, Lucy, and Alice to Martha's Vineyard, where they had a summer home. Now a sedate young lady of nineteen, with long skirts, neatly parted black hair drawn tightly back into a braided pug, she was still at heart the lively, adventurous child.

Thanks to Elizabeth, her skills were many. She was a good pianist, spoke French almost as well as English, loved to read and to cook. No wonder she was always a welcome guest in the homes of all the Blackwells! She liked to visit Henry best, for she and his daughter Alice were closer than sisters. In fact, when Alice was about four, the two had made a pact to become "engaged," and the friendship was to last for the rest of their lives.

Elizabeth's trip was no holiday. Anna was too grief stricken. But her visit in Paris resulted in one interesting happening.

"You remember your old friend Hippolyte Blot?" asked Anna casually. "I have met him and his wife sometimes. I thought you might like to renew your friendship, so we are driving to his home this afternoon."

"Oh— no!" Elizabeth wanted to cry out. She felt as if an old wound, long healed and forgotten, had begun to twinge. But she made ready for the visit, dressing carefully in her best black silk, ribboned bonnet and shawl. Almost surprised, she noticed the change sixteen years had made in her since she had seen him—the graying waves of hair, the careworn face, the unsightly staring glass eye.

But she need not have worried. Hippolyte also had changed, he had become a successful, slightly bald, very respectable doctor.

"*Mon amie, je suis heureux!* (My friend, I am happy!)" he greeted her as any polite French gentleman might have done. They talked pleasantly of old times, their careers, recent discoveries in medicine, especially the experiments of the French scientist Louis Pasteur.

Elizabeth was amused, stimulated, but she felt no romantic emotion. She liked his polite, intelligent wife and his two charming children, but she did not even think, "I might be in her place. They might be my children." She and Hippolyte were just two old friends, two doctors sharing mutual ideas. She was glad when it came time to go home.

Elizabeth returned to her home, infirmary, and the problems that seemed to come with them. Alice lived with them at the infirmary that year of 1867, while Henry and Lucy were traveling in the West campaigning for the vote for women, for Henry was as dedicated as Lucy in fighting for women's rights. Kitty was amused because Alice actually trembled with awe in the presence of Aunt Elizabeth.

"I know she's kind and wouldn't hurt anybody," confessed nine-year-old Alice, "and she's almost as short as I am, and yet—"

"And yet," admitted Kitty, "sometimes she can look at least six feet tall."

Kitty's summer at Martha's Vineyard in 1868 was almost perfect, for Doctor was here for a while too. In fact, by now the whole family made it their summer home, including Uncle Sam and Aunt Nette and their tribe of five little girls. It was that summer that Kitty felt she had really become a Blackwell, for to Grandma she had become the most important family member. She was the only one who could make Grandma's bed to suit her, the blanket next to her to come up to her shoulders, the next one a little lower, and so on. "I want Kitty to make it," Grandma insisted. "She understands."

But the summer was not perfect. She had noticed that Doctor and Aunt Emily did not always see eye to eye. Everything in the infirmary seemed to be running smoothly. Plans for the medical school were progressing. Doctor seemed very sure how everything should be run, and being older than Aunt Emily and the real head of the work, she usually had her way. But Kitty sensed there was something wrong. Then one day that fall, just before Aunt Marian went to Europe, Kitty overheard the talk between Doctor and Aunt Marian. Kitty did not mean to eavesdrop. She had come in from her singing lesson and was sitting in the attic bedroom next to Doctor's with the door open.

"If Kitty were here," she heard Aunt Marian

say ,"I'd ask her advice about this green merino cloth. She has such good taste."

Kitty was about to tell them she was here, when to her dismay the conversation started. Then it was too late.

"I wonder if you know, Bessie," Aunt Marian was saying, "how much you are alienating Emily. There's something about the way you do things that rubs her the wrong way. You always were very sure of yourself, you know. You're such a— such an intense, determined person! She used to be afraid you might not be able to work well together. I think you ought to know."

Kitty refused to hear any more. Cheeks burning, she clapped her hands over her ears.

20

THE DREAM FULFILLED

The Women's Medical College of the New York Infirmary was opened on November 2, 1868, the result of fifteen years of careful planning, patient work, much faith, and the long tedious raising of nearly thirty thousand dollars.

"It's an easy thing," said Elizabeth in her address to the assembled crowd, "to found a poor college. To found a really good college is difficult." Especially a women's medical college, she told them, because there was so much prejudice against women doctors. They must be trained even better than men. Therefore she planned three winter sessions of five months each, hoping soon to extend them to eight months. This was more than a year longer than had been required at Geneva.

In the climax of her speech, she stressed prevention instead of just cure . . . children born to live, not die . . . the concern women should feel for the terrible death rate among children. The new medical college would become the first school in the world to have a professor of hygiene.

There was plenty of publicity. Cartoonists had great fun picturing women students at work, aprons over hoop skirts, gingerly carving up bodies. Most doctors were shocked by the new features. What! Three sessions of five months each, with a plan of increasing to four, when only two, a total of ten or twelve months, was enough for men students? A chair of hygiene! What on earth was that? Poppycock!

But many of the younger and better trained doctors in New York were willing to serve on the faculty, and of the eleven professors only three were women. Dr. Emily was professor of women's diseases. Elizabeth, of course, taught hygiene.

Another new feature of the college was an examining board to pass on students' completion of their work, long before such a board was required by the state. Of the eight examiners chosen the one person who pleased Elizabeth most was that of Dr. Stephen Smith, her classmate at Geneva, who was a prominent New York doctor, and one of the few who agreed with her on the importance of hygiene. Now, after twenty years, he had surely had his question answered—*what sort of woman?*

They had been able to rent the house next to the infirmary, 128 Second Avenue, for the new school. There were seventeen students in the first class. They studied such subjects as anatomy, physiology, chemistry. The second year they would be taught medicine, surgery, obstetrics. The third year they would actually practice with patients and write reports on the cases they attended.

Elizabeth had accomplished everything she had set out to do. She had succeeded beyond her wildest dreams. Yet if what Marian told her was true, that Emily resented her and felt they did not work in harmony, then she had failed. For a long time after their talk she had been uncertain, hurt, bitter. But as she thought about it, she knew that Marian was right. Emily was by far the more gifted doctor, yet Elizabeth, as the founder of the work, often did assume more authority. The truth came to her like the first hint of winter cold. *She had done her work here. She was no longer needed.*

She wrote about her problem to one of her British friends.

"Come to England," the friend wrote. "You know you always planned to settle here sometime. And we need you desperately. Come and help us do for the women of England what you have done for the women of America."

She was no longer cold. She felt warm with the first breath of coming spring. She was not yet fifty. She would give the rest of her life to the country of her birth, practicing medicine, helping other women to practice it, lecturing, and writing.

Emily seemed aghast at her news. Could Marian have been wrong? Elizabeth knew she had made the right decision.

"Do you really want to go?"

Elizabeth barely hesitated. "Yes," she said firmly. "And I couldn't do it if you weren't here to take over. My work here is done. There's something in me, Milly, that likes to start new things. I guess I was born to be a pioneer."

If she had any regrets they were gone, though she had no idea what the future held in store: that she would help open the medical profession for Englishwomen, aid in founding a hospital and medical college, organize a national health society, and that for forty years she would wage fearless battles against one of the worst social evils in England. She knew only that one era of her life had ended, and another was beginning.

It was an evening in July, 1869. Elizabeth's little

attic room was stifling. Kneeling on the floor, she strained over the straps of a large box filled with leftovers from her trunks. There! Mopping her face, she leaned back and surveyed her baggage. It was done. In the morning the cart would come to take it all to the ship docks. Nothing to do now but to cut the last strings binding her to America.

Quietly she went down the stairs and passed among the beds in the wards, patting a hand here and there, giving a word of comfort or encouragement. Then, nodding to the nurse in charge, she went on downstairs and out of doors.

The neighborhood had changed little since she had first seen it. There were the same molding tenements and refuse-strewn alleys. Her sixteen years here might not have been. No, it was not quite the same. For as she passed, she was recognized. "Look, it's Doctor!" A woman with a smiling face and a healthy child at her breast came down some steps to greet her.

"See, Doctor! My others all die, but this one lives, thanks to you and your hospital!"

A child with a cleaner face than the others ran up and shyly touched her hand.

She stopped in the shadows and looked back at the infirmary. There it was, the result of all her years of struggle, there and in human lives—children with healthier bodies, women with brighter faces, and students for whom she had made the way a bit easier.

She stood looking up at the set of high narrow buildings. How long would her work remain? Ten years? Forty? For forty years Elizabeth would know of her infirmary's wonderful growth. She would be happy that Emily was guiding it with great skill, her students graduating with the highest honors.

But the infirmary remained more than forty. A hundred and more, though she never saw the ten-story, shining white New York Infirmary building which would be built in 1954, or its twelve-story counterpart opened in 1965! How she would have exulted in it all, and especially in the clinics that would put into practice her intense concern for prevention rather than cure. They would have been the fulfillment of all her dreams. Only one detail in that future would have seemed to her unimportant—that all this achievement had resulted from the work of one lone, dedicated woman.

She became suddenly aware that she had been standing gazing for— how long? Coming out of the shadows she moved swiftly along the street. As she hurried past a street lamp a group of rowdy boys passed by. One of them pointed at her and shouted something. She heard just a few of the words.

"See that lone woman walking like mad!"

Elizabeth chuckled. How well it described her! *Lone woman.* What else had she been, in her family, in her classrooms, in the medical profession! And she had certainly gone through life walking like mad!

Chuckling again, she quickened her steps. It was late, and tomorrow was a new day, a new life. She was ready for it.

20

KITTY LOOKS BACK

It was 1910, forty years later. Kitty turned the key and opened the door of Rock House in Hastings, England. It was just as she had left it. In fact, the house had changed little since she and Doctor had taken possession of it one day in March, 1879, with snow falling and a bitter northeast wind blowing. Most people would have been timid about living in this eagle's nest at the top of the West Hill, with a sheer drop on one side of hundreds of feet. But not Doctor, and not Kitty.

Dozens of times in the past thirty years she had been wakened by the shaking of her bed, and been lulled to sleep by the roaring and pounding of the wind. Was it living with Doctor for a half century that made her exult in storms and high places, walking sure-footed along dizzying mountain paths? But there were no winds or storms today. The world outside seemed as barren of life and motion as the house itself.

She still couldn't believe it was true. She wandered through the house as if searching for Doctor in all the most likely places—the four-poster bed, the comfortable chair between the fireplace and book-lined wall, the upstairs

terrace. It was here in Elizabeth's best loved
retreat, looking down over tumbling roofs to the
shimmering harbor, with its bright-sailed fishing
boats, that she finally awoke to the truth. Doctor
was gone. She had laid her to rest just a few days
ago up in Scotland, where she had loved to go.

For fifty-six years Kitty had had no life of her
own apart from Doctor. She had never married or
wanted to. They had been closer than most
mothers and daughters. As one of the Blackwells
had once said, Kitty "had fitted into Elizabeth's
angles and curves like an eiderdown quilt." Now
she felt like that same quilt, emptied, limp,
useless.

Yet she felt relief, too. Doctor had wanted to go.
Her keen mind had become clouded. She had not
been herself since she had fallen down the stairs
in Scotland three years before. There were few
Blackwells left of her generation. Henry and Lucy
were gone, fighting for women's rights to the end.
Sam and Ellen had been gone nine years; Anna,
ten; Marian for three.

But how much progress Doctor had seen in her
ninety years! Not only the growth of her work in
America, but in England the founding of a new
hospital for women and the London School of
Medicine for Women, where she had taught for
many years. She had lived to see 550 names of
women added to her own on the British Medical
Register. Since the discoveries of Lister and
Pasteur her ideas of cleanliness and sanitation
were no longer laughed at. Almost every doctor
accepted them. Her own story of her life, *Pioneer
Work in Opening the Medical Profession to Women,*
was still in print after fifteen years.

It was Kitty who had persuaded her to write her
story. But the last chapter, the last forty years, had

never been written. Not in a book, that is. But words for it were not lacking. They were all about her, here in Rock House, thousands, millions of them, in Doctor's writings and lectures.

In her loneliness Kitty gladly plunged into the task of cleaning, sorting, packing, and preparing to leave for a new life in America with her beloved Alice Stone Blackwell, who had always been dearer than a sister. She sorted, dusted, packed, and nailed the lids on dozens of boxes containing more than eleven hundred books. Some Doctor had written. The titles read like the beat of Doctor's marching feet: *The Religion of Health, Medicine and Morality, Physical Education of Girls, The Human Element in Sex.*

Kitty chuckled. What a furor this last book had caused! How people had shuddered at its frank words about the human body! A dozen publishers had refused to print it, and Elizabeth had finally had it printed at her own expense.

But Doctor had been used to opposition, even abuse. She had always been championing unpopular causes like sickness and old-age insurance, better housing, cooperatives to help the poor buy food at lower prices. It would be many years before many of her dreams would be realized. Yet Doctor had never given up hope.

"The years seem to move more swiftly," she had written Aunt Nette, "and to me more and more joyfully. I work on with clear conviction that good is stronger than evil, and there is a grand moral purpose in creation."

Kitty had a long task at Rock House. Before she completed it news came that Emily had died. But at last the work was finished, the forty years neatly stacked, labeled, and packed away.

What now? There was still Rock House. It

belonged to Kitty. Doctor had deeded it to her
long ago, in 1894, for her security. She would be
glad to leave it. It held too many memories. She
would sell it, but to someone who would love it
and not change it too much, someone who would
be willing to have Doctor remembered by those
who might want to visit it.

Already her friends were talking of a tablet to
be placed on the outside wall in memory of its
famous occupant. Kitty knew the lines she would
have written on it, from a poem by Browning,
revised just a little. Doctor had loved them,
and—none but Kitty could know any better—she
had lived them.

One who never turned her back but marched straight
forward,
    Never doubted clouds would break,
Never dreamed, though right were worsted, wrong
would triumph,
    Held, we fail to rise, are baffled to fight better,
      Sleep to wake.

CHRISTIAN HERALD ASSOCIATION AND ITS MINISTRIES

CHRISTIAN HERALD ASSOCIATION, founded in 1878, publishes The Christian Herald Magazine, one of the leading interdenominational religious monthlies in America. Through its wide circulation, it brings inspiring articles and the latest news of religious developments to many families. From the magazine's pages came the initiative for **CHRISTIAN HERALD CHILDREN** and **THE BOWERY MISSION**, two individually supported not-for-profit corporations.

CHRISTIAN HERALD CHILDREN, established in 1894, is the name for a unique and dynamic ministry to disadvantaged children, offering hope and opportunities which would not otherwise be available for reasons of poverty and neglect. The goal is to develop each child's potential and to demonstrate Christian compassion and understanding to children in need.

Mont Lawn is a permanent camp located in Bushkill, Pennsylvania. It is the focal point of a ministry which provides a healthful "vacation with a purpose" to children who without it would be confined to the streets of the city. Up to 1000 children between the age of 7 and 11 come to Mont Lawn each year.

Christian Herald Children maintains year-round contact with children by means of a *City Youth Ministry.* Central to its philosophy is the belief that only through sustained relationships and demonstrated concern can individual lives be truly enriched. Special emphasis is on individual guidance, spiritual and family counseling and tutoring. This follow-up ministry to inner-city children culminates for many in financial assistance toward higher education and career counseling.

THE BOWERY MISSION, located at 227 Bowery, New York City, has since 1879 been reaching out to the lost men on the Bowery, offering them what could be their last chance to rebuild their lives. Every man is fed, clothed and ministered to. Countless numbers have entered the 90-day residential rehabilitation program at the Bowery Mission. A concentrated ministry of counseling, medical care, nutrition therapy, Bible study and Gospel services awakens a man to spiritual renewal within himself.

These ministries are supported solely by the voluntary contributions of individuals and by legacies and bequests. Contributions are tax deductible. Checks should be made out either to **CHRISTIAN HERALD CHILDREN** or to **THE BOWERY MISSION**.

Administrative Office: 40 Overlook Drive, Chappaqua, New York 10514
Telephone: (914) 769-9000